BALANCING LIFE'S DEMANDS

BALANCING LIFE'S DEMANDS

A New Perspective on
PRIORITIES

J. Grant Howard

MULTNOMAH PRESS
PORTLAND, OREGON 97266

Unless otherwise indicated, all Scripture quotations are from the New American Standard Bible, © 1960, 1962, 1963, 1968, 1971, 1972, 1973, 1975, 1977 by The Lockman Foundation, La Habra, California. Used by permission.

Cover design and photography by Paul Lewis

BALANCING LIFE'S DEMANDS
© 1983 by Multnomah Press
Portland, Oregon 97266

Printed in the United States of America

Library of Congress Cataloging in Publication Data

Howard, J. Grant.
  Balancing life's demands.

   1. Christian life—1960-   I. Title.
BV4501.2.H625   1983   248.4   82-24581
ISBN 0-88070-012-2

86 87 88 89 90 91 92 – 12 11 10 9 8 7 6 5 4 3 2

to
Audrey:
one of
my
top
priorities

Contents

A Study Guide for this book is available through Multnomah Press.

Preface

It can be uncomfortable when a perfectly beautiful theory encounters a group of homely but relevant facts. The traditional approach to priorities is a beautiful theory, an attractive concept. By the traditional approach I mean the view that says God is to have first place in my life, someone else second, another third, and so on.

I would like to confront this traditional view with some relevant, biblical facts. Many of you are comfortable with, even committed to, some form of the traditional approach. I am convinced that many aspects of this approach are unbiblical, illogical, and unworkable. Thus, this encounter may make you uncomfortable!

I am indebted to many colleagues, hundreds of students, and multitudes of lay folk who have helped me interact with these concepts for years. And my thanks to Rebecca Thompson who typed the entire manuscript.

J. Grant Howard

PART 1

A Second Look at Sequential Priorities

CHAPTER ONE

Inundated by Options

It's Thursday. Patricia stands in her closet, deliberating on what dress she'll wear. Fred is picking through his ties, looking for one that will go with his herringbone coat. Son Tim is rummaging through the kitchen cupboard, selecting his breakfast cereal. His sister Tammy is browsing through the morning paper, determining which story she'll cut out and report on to her social sciences class later this morning. Before she leaves for work Patricia selects something from the freezer and leaves it in the sink to thaw for supper. On his way to work Fred checks through the AM radio dial and finally settles on some classical music on one of the FM stations. At lunch Tim hits the local hamburger dispensary and finally decides on #17—the octagon shaped quarter-pounder with alfalfa sprouts and celery hearts on a garbanzo bean bun with dried banana chips.

All day long the family makes decisions: picking and choosing, selecting and rejecting, preferring certain things, passing up others. Why? Because they, like all of us, on Thursdays and every day, are surrounded by a vast array of alternatives.

If life can be viewed as a battle, then here is the latest and most appropriate communique:

We are completely surrounded and totally outnumbered.

That is a realistic progress report from the weary foot soldiers on the front lines of life. Surrounded? Outnumbered? By what?

OPTIONS! In the battle of life we are up against options. Everywhere we turn there are choices to be made. Obligations that pressure us. Opportunities that entice us. We are bombarded with places to go, overrun with people to meet, pinned down with things to buy, fatigued with mail to read. We are being inundated on all sides by powerful forces that clamor for our time, talents, money, influence, wisdom. There is also a psychological aspect to this campaign: We are infiltrated by feelings of guilt because we cannot possibly respond to all the options.

At times we are so pummeled with options that we contemplate surrender. We look in vain for a white flag to wave. Gradually we realize that we are under siege and that the siege lasts a lifetime. We can't surrender. We can't escape. We just keep on fighting. And the fight is carried on by making decisions. Some decisions involve only a minor skirmish; others are major. When we make the right choice, we win. If it's the wrong choice, we lose. There are no cease-fires, and tomorrow there will be more skirmishes.

Let's take a moment to analyze these options more carefully.

Necessary Options

Some options *demand* our attention. We get hungry; eating is a necessary option. We are worn out; the best option is sleep. You look in the mirror and see another day's beard growth. Once again it is necessary to shave. The diaper is wet; the baby lets us know that change is the right option. It will be months before that option dries up!

There are other options that are almost as compelling as eating and sleeping. When the phone rings, we answer it. When there is a knock at the door, we see who it is. When the mail comes, we open it. When April 15 rolls around, we file our tax return. When the early morning alarm rings . . . well, that may not be the best illustration. At any rate, life has for each of us a set of things we consider imperative. They have to be done. We do them.

Postponable Options

A lot of things don't put such stringent demands on us. We can put them off for awhile. Or we can avoid them altogether. The dishes ought to be done, but they don't have to be. It would be nice to wash the car, change the oil, tune the engine, and rotate the tires on a regular basis. But your car will run a long way with mud on the hood, dirt in the crankcase, a miss in the engine, and uneven wear on the tires. You may end up walking, but in the interim you had time for things you deemed more important.

You should write or call the folks, but you don't have to. You ought to study for the test, but you can cram later, or wing it. Now would be a good time to express your appreciation, but you can wait, and forget. It would be good to play with your kids now, but you can sidestep it for the present. That's the way life is. Some things seem to have a way of requiring our attention. Other things request our attention, but don't demand it. Many things can be put off indefinitely.

Bad Options

Options have moral implications. There are plenty of options to do the wrong thing. Let's start early in the morning. Tony's alarm goes off, inconsiderately interrupting his dreams, calling him to consciousness. Still semi-conscious, he sneaks his hand out from under the covers and conducts an extensive search of the top of the bedside table, working over the blanket control and the phone before he finally discovers and silences the alarm. Now Tony has the option of rolling over and sleeping in. That could be the wrong choice. Or Tony can come out of the sack grumbling and griping, letting everyone in the house know in his inimitable way that "grouchy" is up and needs to be coddled. A wrong option. He's late, so he drives too fast to work. Another bad option. He promises a customer delivery sooner than it is possible. Not good. He makes another appointment on top of an already overloaded schedule. Bad. He eats too much for lunch. Bad. He pads his expense account. Poor move. Tony, and any of us, can muddle through a day choosing the wrong options time and time again. They are not always labeled, so we have to learn to discern and sort out the good and the bad. There are a lot of bad options—more than any of us realize.

Good Options

Mixed in with the bad options are a veritable galaxy of good options. I love to read. There are lots of good books to read. I love woodworking tools. There are always plenty of good tools available—on sale! Life offers us a rich selection of good opportunities, good products, and yes, good attitudes and good actions. The selection of good options is not simply abundant, it is unlimited.

What we need to be able to do first is separate the good from the bad. Then we need to take the abundant supply of good options and decide *which ones we can't do!* You see, if a little good is good, then a lot of good is better. Right? Not necessarily so. Operating on this premise, we may easily get caught up in a deceptive process because requests will always outnumber resources. Just about the time you have committed all your money and expended all your energy and filled all your schedule you will look up to see another wave of requests headed your way.

Take today's mail, for example. It contained letters from four legitimate nonprofit organizations asking for money. My heart says yes. My budget says no. I must face the fact that there will always be more good causes than I can afford to support. I enjoy public speaking engagements. When requests come my way to speak, I am sorely tempted to accept every one of them. Saying yes to everyone may be good for my ego but it may be bad for my health, my nerves, my wife, my kids. I need to remind myself of Howard's law:

Requests will always exceed resources.

Doing good is imperative. Doing everything is impossible.

Expanding Options

Our options are proliferating. We have *more* of everything. Have you been to a newsstand recently? There are more magazines on more topics than ever before. Then add to these popular periodicals the profuse supply of technical journals and you can see why we are in an "information explosion." As a result, we have more to look at, browse through, read, study, and learn. This flourishing print media exposes us to new options in ideas. The advertising contained therein exposes us to new options in products and better options in prices. Movies, radio, and television contribute powerfully to the expanding of these options.

Technology has been a driving force behind this explosion of options. It has given us jet aircraft, which have increased our options for travel. It has provided computers and word processors, which have multiplied our options in handling numbers and words. It has put microwave ovens into our kitchens. Hasn't that increased your cooking options? Hasn't the recreational vehicle fostered new options for vacations? Hasn't the day-and-night electronic bank teller inaugurated new options for depositing, withdrawing, and spending? How about the church? Does it have a creative program that challenges its people with new options for growth and service?

Every day new selections are added to life's catalog of options. We must decide which we will incorporate into our lives and which we will leave out. Our "choosers" are being challenged like never before. That's why we say we are not only surrounded but outnumbered. No one has been able to declare a moratorium on the proliferation of options.

Deceptive Options

At first glance many options are exciting and enticing. But live with them for awhile and the luster wears off. You accepted the promotion, but now you are struggling with longer hours and greater responsibility. The product was on sale and you convinced yourself that you had to have it. Now you are making monthly payments on it and wondering what kind of mental gymnastics you engaged in to con yourself into thinking you couldn't live without it.

Travel is a deceptive option. I always thought it would be great to travel hither and yon, speaking to groups of admiring people. It is great. It is also boring and exhausting. Many people desperately want the option of owning their own business. If they do reach that goal, they discover all the hidden responsibilities that go with being their own boss. Sex without marriage is an available, but deceptive option. Retirement—with "nothing to do"—is a deceptive option.

Deception doesn't always hide just the negatives. I really didn't know what I was getting into when I bought a radial arm saw a few years ago. Since then I have been discovering the rich variety of jobs you can do with it. Perhaps you, on occasion, have been pushed into a relationship with a new roommate or locker partner. At first it didn't seem too appealing or profitable, but the more you developed it, the better it got. The point is this: Many options are not transparent. They need to be explored and evaluated with care. What you see is not always what you get.

Motivating Options

Options aren't passive. Nor are they neutral. They actively persuade us to respond. We aren't passive or neutral either. We want to be successful and effective. Put aspiring people in the context of stimulating options and what do you have? Motivation!

We live under pressure: pressure to conform, to perform, to create, to commit. Much of this pressure is healthy for us. It instigates personal growth and achievement. Some of it is bad for us. It generates winds that may blow us off course, or overboard.

The company issues this challenge: "Do a good job and you will be rewarded accordingly." That is an option that motivates employees to excel, and they seek to find other options that will help them do a good job. There is the option of coming a bit early, the option of working overtime, the option of taking a briefcase full of work home for the evening, the option of taking courses at the local college. These are strong options, because they could secure for you a raise and a promotion. Furthermore, they give you the inner satisfaction of being successful and effective.

However, the very same options that impress your boss may irritate your spouse. So we have to be very, very careful not to allow the motivating potential of options to throw us all out of balance and jeopardize other significant relationships. Options are complex and so are we. They have the capacity to drive us to use more and more of our potential—and that may be good. Yet they also have the capacity to blind us to all of the consequences of choosing certain options—and that can be bad.

There is a sense in which the world is designed to extract every ounce of potential from us. We place similar demands within ourselves. Motivated by internal and external forces, we run to win. But we must be cautious. The legitimate desire for excellence can easily drive us to excess.

The Problem

We are surrounded by innumerable options. Gathered around each of us is a massive array of alternatives. Some must be done, others can be put off. Some are bad, others are good. Some tend to deceive us. Others try to motivate us. And the supply is ever-increasing—tending to overwhelm us. We are overstimulated, overchallenged, overexposed. And if we don't watch out, we can become overcommitted.

What is the answer? Some vow to do little or nothing and seek, in some serene way, to drop out of any vital, active, productive lifestyle. Others frantically try to respond to nearly every stimulus and in the process become prime candidates for a breakdown. There must be a better way.

The Solution

The answer? PRIORITIES! The solution to our schizophrenic schedules is to establish the proper priorities. If we are going to get out of the rat race and live relaxed, normal lives, then we have to get our priorities straight. If we are going to accurately handle the barrage of options coming our way every day, then we must have a workable list of priorities. We desperately need an adequate grid through which we can screen the incessant demands on our time and talents.

How do you spell relief? P-R-I-O-R-I-T-I-E-S. Sounds good. Let's see how we go about this.

By the Way . . .

Are you sure you have time to read this book right now? Shouldn't you be off doing something else? You have bills to pay and the bank statement to balance. You need to put the dirty clothes in the washer and run to the store. You probably should play with the kids and then watch that special on television. It would be good to call Anne. And get started on your homework.

Aren't you leaving a lot of important things undone in order to read this book? How can you justify such behavior? I mean, with all the various pressures of life flooding in on you, how in the world can you sit around and read a book! It would appear you have decided at this point in time that this book is an option taking priority over everything else in your life. How did you arrive at that conclusion?

CHAPTER TWO

Life by the List

"Good morning," said the teacher enthusiastically.

"Good morning," responded the group, a bit half-heartedly, not because it wasn't a good morning and not because they weren't glad to be there, but simply because they had no leader to orchestrate a resounding, unified response.

"For those of you who haven't met me, I'm Jack Todd. As you know, I'm filling in for Don Brinkman, who is on vacation. Don told me to teach on any subject I wanted, so I think we'll deal with priorities. I struggle with priorities in my own life and I have a hunch you do too. So let's have a go at it and see how far we can get."

"Priority," he said, writing it on the overhead projector, and then focusing the word clearly on the screen. "What does that mean? Well, *prior* means earlier in time or order—so if something takes priority, it means that it merits prior attention, it comes before, it takes precedence. Or could we even say that it is more important than something else? Let's put it this way: Priorities mean that something is more important than something else; or one thing is more important than another thing.

"Okay, the question we want to deal with today is: What is more important than what? What are a Christian's main priorities and what order should we put them in? To facilitate your immediate thinking on this I'm going to pass out an Agree/Disagree sheet. As soon as you get yours, go to work on it. Read each statement to yourself and then check whether you agree or disagree. It may be difficult, but see if you can commit yourself on each one."

What's More Important Than What?

Statement	Agree	Disagree
1. My relationship with God is more important than my relationship with other people.	☐	☐
2. The Bible teaches that my relationships with Christians are more important than my relationships with non-Christians.	☐	☐
3. It is more important for the Christian to witness than to eat.	☐	☐
4. My family responsibilities are more important than my church responsibilities.	☐	☐
5. My responsibility to myself is not as important as my responsibility to others.	☐	☐
6. Bible study and prayer are the most important responsibilities the Christian has.	☐	☐
7. It is more important to spend time with my wife/husband than to spend time studying the Bible.	☐	☐
8. I discharge my biblical responsibilities properly by devoting the right amount of time to each one.	☐	☐
9. Putting God first in my life means putting someone else last.	☐	☐

"Okay, time's up." Jack Todd spent the next few minutes finding out where the group stood on each of the nine statements. On some there was obvious agreement by nearly everyone. On other statements, the group was split right down the middle. Frequently, the group broke into Jack's informal poll with comments. Many felt the statements were too vague for them to commit themselves to a definite agree or disagree response.

"All right," Jack said. "That stimulated our thinking in the realm of priorities. Now let's personalize all of this and figure out what our priorities are. We'll list them on the screen." He poised his pen at the ready. "What comes first? Who is number one?"

A number of people quickly volunteered what everyone knew to be the obvious and correct answer. "God."

"You want to put God first? You all agree with that? Any other nominations?"

"I move that nominations cease," said Charlie, the class joker, "and that God be elected by acclamation. All in favor say aye."

"Aye," came the resounding response, accompanied by chuckles.

"Okay, God has been unanimously elected to first place on our priority list. I'm sure He will accept the position. God is on top. He is Number One. I think every Christian group would agree. Well, that's settled. Now who's next? Who is number two?" Jack looked out at the group.

Silence. People were thinking it over, trying to come up with the best answer. Finally, a woman spoke.

"Well, next to God I'd put . . . my husband." A roar of laughter went up from the class.

Red faced, the woman continued. "Now wait a minute! Let me clarify. I don't mean that he is almost as good as God. What I mean is that if God is the most important person in my life, then my husband is the next in importance. He is number two."

"I'll vote for that," said her husband, "and furthermore, I'd put her in the same position in my life. The way marriage is deteriorating today, we really need to give it a high priority."

"And the way families are falling apart, we need to give

our children high priority, too," chimed in another member.

"Right," Jack agreed. "Now it seems like we are developing a consensus and that most everybody is comfortable with marriage and family—or the home—occupying second place on our priority list. Let's use the word "family" to include all of these relationships in the home." He wrote *family* on the screen in bold letters, just below *God*. "The family needs attention and putting it second on the list gives it high visibility. By the way, how do you put God *ahead* of your family? And how do you put family *after* God? These are interesting questions . . . but our top priority right now is to establish our list, so we'll have to bypass them for the time being."

Jack glanced up. "I see a hand back there. Yes, right there. What's that? Oh, you're single and want to know where you fit in; that is, what number two on the list is for you. What do you think, class?"

There was a quick response from the rest of the group.

"Singles get a wild card. They get to pick a priority, any priority, and place it in the number two slot."

"Singles get to hold number two open for emergencies."

"It looks like singles don't have a number two."

"Sure they do. They have parents, brothers, sisters. That's family."

"If you have to be married to have a number two priority, then what about widows, teenagers, divorcees, and even children?"

Jack held up a hand to get everyone's attention. "Well, those are interesting questions and comments. This whole subject of priorities is getting more complex by the moment. It's good to raise these questions, but we can't deal with all of them now. I think we all agree that the family is strategically important, and at the same time, in our present day, the family has many different designs. So, when we say the family is number two, that means different things to different people, depending on their marital and family status.

"Shall we proceed? It's time for number three. How many say *church?*" Jack quickly counted the raised hands. "How many say *work?* How many say *witness?*" He made a quick calculation. "You know what? We have ourselves a real dilemma. A three-way tie for third place. Let's vote again and maybe some will switch." Jack conducted another quick poll.

"Okay. Some of you saw the light and changed your vote. We have a winner—the church! So let's put it up on our list. The third priority is the church." A waving hand caught his attention.

"You have a comment?"

"Yes, actually it's a question, I guess. Shouldn't the church come before the home? It seems to me that a strong church will equip its young people for good marriage and family living, and that to ensure this we ought to give the church a higher priority than number three. It is conceivable to me that you could spend so much time and energy developing your marriage and family that you might not have much time left for the church. Maybe we have it backwards."

Jack nodded. "That's an interesting point. Yet couldn't we also say that strong homes make strong churches? Looks like what we may have is some kind of mutually supportive relationship. Let's leave it this way for the time being. Is there another question?"

A well-dressed man seated about halfway back rose to his feet.

"Yes. We've tossed this phrase around all morning, and I'm just wondering what it means. What does it mean to 'put the church third'?"

"Well, I guess it means that after you have taken care of God and your family then you go to church, or you, uh, direct your attention to the church," Jack replied.

"That raises another question in my mind. What does it mean to 'take care of God'? I know I'm supposed to take care of my family, but how am I supposed to take care of God? Can't God take care of Himself!"

Jack smiled. "No, to take care of God is just another way of saying 'to put God first.' "

"Well, okay," the man persisted, "I think I know what it means to put God first, but I still don't have a very good handle on putting the church third. You said it means to 'direct your attention' to the church. Somebody could interpret that to mean that you face toward the church periodically, like the Moslems do toward Mecca!"

"Well, obviously that's not what we mean. I'm not sure I know precisely what we *do* mean and I'm beginning to wonder why I told Don Brinkman I would teach this class! You ask so many questions. Save them for Don or the pastor. Let's go on and see if we can finish our list.

"Where were we? Oh yes, fourth. What shall it be—work or witness? That ought to be fairly easy. We have to work in order to witness. Besides, doing my job well is one way to witness. That would seem to clinch it. Work is number four on the list."

"Unless you are a pastor or missionary," said someone. "Then your work is your witness and you combine four and five."

"Which reminds me of the saying," Charlie said, clowning again, "that pastors and missionaries are paid to be good, but laymen are good for nothing!"

"Charlie, you have just proved your point! All right, work is fourth on the list and that would put witness right next to it—fifth on the list. Some might make a case for your testimony being more important than your job, but you have to provide for your family, and you can't feed your kids on tracts, unless of course you sell them. The tracts, not the kids!" Still another waving hand caught Jack's attention. "One more question, right back there."

"Yes, in my humble opinion, we are getting everything out of order. Witnessing should be number one. That's every believer's prime responsibility and that is the way we put God first. By actively, aggressively witnessing."

"That's a good thought, but if you push that to its extreme, which could be easily done, then you end up neglecting God, neglecting your family and your job, and even neglecting relationships and responsibilities in your local church. Now, our time is about up. We have five key areas on our priority list. Do we need to add anything else? Seems to me that we are leaving one key person out. What do you think, Fred?"

Fred scratched his head. "Well," he said, "I've been sitting here all morning wondering about myself."

"A lot of us have been wondering about you, Fred! No—just kidding. You mean where to put yourself on the list?"

"Precisely. I suppose, if I am on the list at all, I should

be last. That would seem to be the humble thing to do."

"I'm really glad you brought that up, Fred. It's hard to decide where we fit on a priority list. Some say that a proper view of humility and self-denial means we should leave ourselves off the list. But there seem to be times when we have to pay attention to ourselves. For example, we have to eat and sleep and stay as healthy as we can. I don't see how we can leave ourselves off the list entirely. Let's say we're last but not least. So, there's our list. The sanctified six."

Jack looked up as a tall, graying man slipped into the classroom. "Well, look who's here. We could say he's late for this class or early for the next service . . . but let's give him the benefit of the doubt and classify him as early for worship. Ted, we've been working on our list of personal priorities. Here they are: God, family, church, work, witness, and self."

"Sounds good," Ted agreed. "But isn't it a bit complex and confusing? I operate on a simple, clear approach I learned years ago: JOY—Jesus, others, you."

"That is a simple approach. And you are right, Ted. Setting up priorities is a confusing and complex task. We left a lot of unanswered questions in our discussion today. But at least we have a good list to help us evaluate and plan our day-to-day activities." Jack glanced at his watch. "Okay, it's time to go. Be here next Sunday."

By the Way . . .

How does the above list compare with yours? Different order? Different items? If you have a list of priorities, how did you arrive at it? Did you get it from your pastor? Your church? Did some speaker develop it for you? Was it presented in a book or a seminar or a workshop? Did you develop it on your own?

The question of where you got it is not nearly as significant as the question of what it means. What does it mean to put God first? What does it mean to put family second? What does it mean to put self last? What does it mean to prioritize your life? Read on!

CHAPTER THREE

Probing the Sequential Approach

Being an engineer with an analytical mind, Tom had been thinking all week about last Sunday's class on priorities. He was uneasy about the fact that so many questions had been left unanswered. And he was especially stimulated by the questions about what it means to put God first. Some of you are no doubt pondering this, too, so let's dive right in and squarely face the issue.

God First?

What does it mean to put God first? That's a good question. Everybody uses the phrase, "put God first," but nobody explains it. Why not? Because it's obvious, isn't it? You just put God first. Isn't that clear?

Frankly, no. It is extremely vague and nebulous. I have no clear idea what it means. It could mean any one of a number of things. Taken literally it could mean that if you were making up a list of your favorite people, God would be first on it. Is that what it means? We carry a piece of paper around and look at it now and then to remind ourselves that God is at the top of our list. Or sign it and post it in some prominent place to let others know where God stands, as far as we are concerned.

No, there is more to it than that. It means that each day when you get up, the first thing you do is read your Bible and pray. This means you are putting God first on your daily schedule. He is the first one you talk to and the first one you listen to. The first one you consult with. Not a bad idea.

Suppose, however, that you have this conversation with God at night before you go to bed. Does this mean that you are putting God last? Or could it be that you are putting God first, but your day starts the night before? Or say that you have your devotions at noon. Does this mean you have put God somewhere in the middle? Or is He still first, but your day starts at noon? Suppose you get up late and rush off to work one day without having some time with God. Does this mean God is out of the picture and your priorities are a mess and there is no way for you to live for Him that day?

"Wait a minute!" you say. "I thought I understood it, but the more you explain it, the more confused I get. Clarify!"

That will come later. Let's probe some more.

Marsha is a growing Christian looking for answers to these same questions. Let's eavesdrop on a conversation she is having with herself.

"Well, Marsha, how much time do you need to spend with God in Bible study and prayer to be classified as one who puts God first?"

"Fifteen minutes?"

"That sounds like token commitment."

"How about thirty minutes?"

"That's better, but it still smacks of a qualified first. How about really putting Him first—with all your heart and soul and mind—unqualified first place. Okay, now, how much time are you going to devote to the Word and prayer in a given day?"

"All morning?"

"Come on now, we're talking about unreserved commitment. Really being sold out. Full bore. Fanaticism!"

"All day?"

"Now you're cooking on all four burners! But you're still holding back a bit. Need to light the oven, too.

"All day and night?"

"Right on! Twenty-four hours a day in the Word and prayer. That's what it means to put God first."

Or does it? As they say, when someone gets a good idea, someone else carries it too far. That's what has happened here. All of a sudden we have moved from glorious commitment to spiritual stupidity. If you spend twenty-four hours a day in the Word and prayer, you'll neglect a lot of other important things that need to be done the same day.

Okay, if putting God first doesn't mean placing God at the top of the list or at the beginning of the day, then what exactly is involved? Try this one on for size. It means that I always think about God before I do something. Before I start the car, I think about God. Before I back out of the driveway, I consider God. While I am shopping, I think about God (at least for purchases of ten dollars or more). These things may be true once in awhile, but before I start the car, I always put on my seat belt. Before I back out of the driveway, I look for other cars, kids, and dogs. Before I buy I think about my bank account. Putting God first doesn't mean that I am always thinking about God.

Maybe it means that I always consult God when making major decisions. But what, pray tell, constitutes a major decision? Last week I bought a zoom lens for my camera. It cost nearly $200. Was that a major decision? If so, how does one "consult God" on zoom lenses? I also bought a roll of film for $3. Was that a minor decision? How does one "leave God out" of that minor decision? Would the two purchases be viewed differently if I were a millionaire, or broke, or if I didn't own a camera?

I think you can see that trying to link God only to major decisions is fraught with problems, especially when the Bible says that everything can be done to the glory of God, and that even our careless words are to be accounted for in the judgment (1 Corinthians 10:31, Matthew 12:36).

What then, does putting God first mean? That I engage in certain religious activities? That I put my time into prayer, Scripture reading, meditation, memorization, and attending church services? But here we are forced back to a basic question: How much is enough? How much Scripture do I have to memorize to assure God of first place? If I quote a verse incorrectly, does that drop Him out of first place? How many services do I have to attend to put God first? How much money do I have to give to put God first? How long do I have to meditate to let God know He is number one? Furthermore, are any of these activities exclusively God-centered? Aren't self and others involved, too?

This is confusing, you say. I agree. Religious people tend to latch on to certain clichés and repeat them over and over until they think they know what they mean. Maybe they do, but in the event we—or others—don't, we need to work constantly at simplifying and clarifying our religious jargon.

"Putting God first" is a nebulous, potentially confusing cliché. I suggest we excise it. Or if we must keep it, let's invest it with biblical, practical meaning. This is one of our goals in this book.

Family Second?

Putting the family second is a phrase just as fuzzy. When we aren't clear on what it means to put God first, then how can we ever be clear on what it means to put the family second? If you don't understand basic math, you sure can't handle calculus. But let's give it a try.

Time. That's it. Less time to the family than you give to God, but more time to the family than you give to the church. Is that the way you put the family second? (A thought: if priority means time, and God is first, wouldn't we spend *all* our time with God?)

No, says someone else, it is the quality of time, not just the amount of time. Does this mean you give the highest quality time to God and then just a little bit lesser quality time to the family? No, of course not! Then maybe what you mean is that when you get up in the morning the first thing you do is talk with God and the second thing you do is talk with the family.

So Pete struggles out of bed at 6:00 A.M. and spends one hour of quality time listening and talking to God (provided, of course, that chronobiologically his circadian cycle peaks in the early morning so he can give God the highest quality time he is capable of giving!). At 7:00 he wakes Madge and the kids, assembles them in the family room, and engages in forty-five minutes (God gets an hour because He's first) of dialogue designed to maintain them in second place. God takes Saturday off, so everyone sleeps in. On Sunday, Pete and Madge put God first by attending the early worship service.

The family remains solidly in second place by going to Sunday school *after* the worship hour. . . . I agree with you; none of this really seems to capture the concept of second place. Instead, it borders on the ridiculous.

Could it be that we should give our families attention worthy of second place? In competition, first place gets a gold medal. Second place gets silver. Same size but different color and content. Does this analogy help? Give God and family their properly deserved and different kinds of attention. God deserves our best—gold. Family gets the next best—silver. God always wins. That's good. The family never wins. That's good?

Another real problem is determining when I have discharged my responsibility to God and can begin to work on second place responsibilities to the family. At what point have I finished putting God first? I need to know this so I'll know at what point I can begin work on my family.

Pete needs to know it too. Is 6:00 early enough? Is an hour long enough? Is five out of seven mornings consistent enough? Is Pete's knowledge of Scripture broad enough? Is his fellowship with the Father deep enough? If not, should he spend less time with the family and more time with God, until God is firmly established in first place? When and how does God notify Pete about all of this?

No, you say, that is simply not the issue at all. If we set up priorities and label them as first, second, third, and so on, then we have to live life in sequence, and that's not the way we live. Life is lived in situations. You don't sequence your priorities, you situationalize them. And furthermore, any situation can potentially involve God. Unless we insist on isolating God in first place.

Church Third?

How do you put church *after* family? Give to the church after you have bought what the family needs? Go to church after you have done what needs to be done for your mate and your children? Think about these questions. Analyze them carefully. Because if we are going to put the family second and the church third, then we must take steps to accomplish this feat. If you analyze these two questions carefully, you'll find that they are loaded with enigmas and paradoxes. There is a sense in which they don't make sense!

How do you go about putting the church third? What does third mean? Does it involve certain attendance factors; certain service requirements; a certain level of giving; certain types of serving, attending, and fulfilling certain duties? If you go on vacation for a couple of weeks in the summer, you couldn't put the church third during that time. When you get back must you devote more time to the church to bring it back into balance? If family responsibilities have been neglected, would you be allowed to sideline church for awhile in order to work on family priorities? Which is worse: a church split or a family split? Which is most important: personal devotions, family devotions, or a Sunday morning worship service? Are you getting the picture? Sequential priorities are not the answer to our dilemma. "Putting the church third" cries out for clarification.

Work Fourth?

Work is surely not fourth on the priority list in terms of time spent on the job. Most people work an eight-hour day. That could be more time than we give to God, family, and church combined. Perhaps, then, we need to cut back on work hours. But that would lower our incomes so we couldn't provide for family and couldn't give to the church, and that is not giving them their proper priority. Better stick with the eight-hour day.

Mary, a housewife and mother of three young children, doesn't work outside the home. But she works long and hard in the home. Is that her job or her family responsibility? It would seem that family and work are combined for the mother and housewife. Unless she is praying all day in order to put God first!

Or how about Jack, who works ten to twelve hours each day so he can generate more income so he can provide nicer things for his wife and kids and give more to his church. He may be neglecting his family by the lack of his physical presence as he attempts to meet his family's needs for material possessions.

Phil travels a lot. In order to do his job well he has to be gone frequently from his family and his church. Is Phil giving work a higher priority than it merits? Or what about single men and women? Do they move work and church up on the priority scale because certain family responsibilities are non-existent for them?

How do we put work *after* church? Always attend church socials instead of office parties? Turn down opportunities for overtime in order to serve on church committees? Study the Sunday school lesson instead of preparing for the sales meeting? Develop friendships with church members instead of with fellow workers?

Facetious, you say. Ridiculous, I say. God never intended us to ask questions like I am asking, because God never intended us to set up priorities in a one-two-three-four list.

Witness Fifth?

After you have studied the Scriptures and prayed, attended to the needs of your mate and children, rendered appropriate services to the church, and finished your eight-hour shift, *then* you can witness. Right? No, you say, that's not it at all. You witness all the time. In the home, in the church, on the job, everywhere you go, potentially to everyone you meet, possibly in everything you do and say.

Then why give it priority five? Why put it way down on the list, next to last? Is it because other things are more important? What could be more important than the salvation of a human being?

How do you put witness *after* work? Do you share Christ with fellow workers after you have reached a certain level of skill or a certain level of pay? Share Christ with fellow workers after you have demonstrated that you are a competent, loyal, dependable worker? Or do you share Christ with them after your eight-hour shift on the way home in the car pool? Saying that witnessing must come after work is like saying that breathing must come after swallowing. Sometimes it does; sometimes it doesn't. One thing is sure: You have to do both! The analogy breaks down at this point, because you can't breathe and swallow at the same time. You can work and witness at the same time. So, to put witness in fifth place could be both unbiblical and impossible.

Self Last?

Any good ideas as to what "self last" is supposed to mean? Does it mean I give myself time if there is any time left over after the other five areas are handled properly? Talk to myself after I have said all that needs to be said in all the other relationships? Or does it mean in essence that I am not to give myself any attention whatsoever; that *last* essentially means off the list? The only reason for my existence, then, is to fulfill all the other priorities.

Anyone can fall into this "self last" approach to life. Rev. B. A. Servant misses meals in order to counsel, stays up late in order to study, gets up early in order to go to another meeting, and in doing all of this sacrifices his physical well-being on the altar of service. And for some strange reason feels good about feeling bad. A young mother can do the same thing, giving herself so unreservedly to her new baby that she neglects many of her own personal needs. A student can starve himself emotionally, socially, and physically—putting himself last in these areas while his intellectual development reigns supreme. Perhaps the epitome of "self-lastism" is I. M. Humble, the person who firmly believes that humility, obscurity, and inferiority are synonymous.

Actually, we really can't leave ourselves off the list. Think how much time you devote to yourself each day. Six to eight hours to sleep, two to three hours to eat, an hour to groom, some time to read, watch television, relax, visit, shop, jog, hunt, fish, travel. If priority is based on time spent—then you are number one!

Maybe you need to spend less time eating, sleeping, grooming, reading—less time doing the things that are oriented around your own needs—in order to firmly establish yourself in last place on the priority poll. But then, again, you need to sleep more, eat better, and relax more regularly in order to be able to attend to all of your other important priorities. Some say we need to get ourselves out of the picture so God can really work. Others say we are a vital part of the picture, in which God is at work and wants to work.

By the Way . . .

How do you feel about this whole discussion? I have a hunch some of you are frustrated. Some are amused. Some are mad. Some of you are confused. Do you feel your position has been misrepresented? Overstated? Well, if I have stimulated your thinking in the area of sequential priorities, I have accomplished my purpose.

Let me make my point patently clear: A list of priorities doesn't make sense! It can't be intelligently explained. It can't be easily understood. It can't be logically lived out. No matter how you define and describe your particular approach, if it is a sequential approach, it is loaded with contradictions, complexities, confusion, and chaos.

What is the solution? Refine and revamp the existing sequential model? I think not. I am convinced that the existing sequential model is not only impractical but unbiblical. I am also convinced that there *is* a priority model in Scripture. Read on!

PART 2

A Fresh Look at Scripture

CHAPTER FOUR

A Prime Passage on Priorities

Years ago I began searching through Scripture looking for a passage containing foundational truths that would help me deal with the subject of priorities. I found it! It is not the only text but it is a good one. The passage is Matthew 22:34-40. In this incident one of the Pharisees asked Christ a question, and the answer He gave provides, I believe, a framework upon which we can build a basic, biblical doctrine of priorities.

Follow along with me as we probe this passage for "top priority truth."

The Interpretation of Matthew 22:34-40

The Questioner

As I examine the text, the first thing I want to know is *who asked the question?* The source of the question was a Pharisee who was an expert in the Old Testament (22:34-35). He spent his time studying the meaning and relative importance of each of the commandments in the Old Testament. He had 613 of them classified: 248 positive, 365 negative, some great, some small, some heavy, some light. He was ardently devoted to hair-splitting legalism and could carry on lengthy debates about the interpretation and significance of each of the commandments. Hence the question: "Teacher, which is the great commandment in the Law?"

The Motive

Why did he ask the question? To see if he could do better than the Sadducees, who had just tried to put Christ in a bad light and had ended up there themselves (22:23-33). Also, he wanted to test Christ (22:35); in other words, to pose a question that would be difficult to answer and easy to argue about. Though his motives were probably not the purest, it is clear from the parallel account of this incident in Mark's gospel that his attitude was not totally negative (Mark 12:28-34).

The Question

Having probed the Pharisee's motives, we are now ready to find out *what question did he ask?* "Teacher, which is the great commandment in the Law?" Of all the 613 commandments, which one is the greatest—which one takes top priority? Jewish rabbis often discussed the various commandments, and the question of which one was most important frequently came up. Now they sought Christ's opinion.

The Answer

What was Christ's answer? "You shall love the Lord your God with all your heart, and with all your soul, and with all your mind" (22:37). Quoting from Deuteronomy 6:5, Christ said that this is the most important commandment—the injunction to man to be involved in a total love commitment to God.

Let's keep probing. *How did Christ classify this commandment?* "This is the great and foremost commandment" (22:38). *Great* and *foremost* are the two words used to impress His listeners with the fact that loving God is the commandment with the highest rank.

We're not through yet. *What other commandment did Christ add?* "You shall love your neighbor as yourself" (22:39). Quoting Leviticus 19:18, Christ added a second commandment to go along with the first. We are to love God and our neighbor—neighbor being that human being who is near and/or of whom we are aware. [1] The quality of this love is expressed in the phrase *as yourself.* Regardless of who this person is, I am to love him or her in the same positive, caring manner that I would treat myself. [2]

Now notice something very significant. *How did Christ classify this commandment?* He classified it as a "second" commandment which was "like" the one He had just mentioned. *Second* does not mean second in importance, for these two commandments are not being ranked, but listed.[3] *Like* links the two commandments together as being of equal and related importance. [4]

The word *like* is important. *In what ways is the second commandment "like" the first?* *Like* is best interpreted as referring to the words immediately preceding, and thus the second commandment is "like" the first commandment in that it too is the "great and foremost commandment" (22:38). "In effect, then, the scribe is being told that no *one* commandment can be marked as 'first,' but that these two together . . . constitute the essence of the law."[5] It is also obvious that the second is like the first in that both involve love, both involve self, both are Old Testament concepts, and both focus on someone beyond self. Though different in direction, the two commandments are quite similar in many respects, and are said to be equal in importance.

The last verse in this section is a powerful, reinforcing summary. *What does verse 40 tell us about these two commandments?* "On these two commandments depend the whole Law and the Prophets." *Depend* can be translated *hang* or *suspend.* The point is that these two commandments are the nail or hook from which you can hang all of the Old Testament. These two statements constitute and summarize the essence of the Law. They "provide the decisive word about its *meaning* and thus enable its correct interpretation."[6] Not only are they both of supreme importance, but they are integrally related to each other and to the rest of the Old Testament.

A Summary of Matthew 22:34-40

What have we learned? The essence of the Bible's teaching and of man's responsibility is contained in these two commandments—love God and love your neighbor. If less were involved, the Lord would have left something out. If more were involved, the Lord would have included it. What we have is a clear, concise statement of what is really important in life.

According to the text, these two commandments are

equal in importance. "The 'second' commandment is not of 'second importance.' It is simply the second of two mentioned as together comprising the 'chief' commandment."[7] The supreme quality and character of the second commandment is "like" that of the first.[8] The Pharisee asked for one commandment. The Lord in essence is saying that it takes two commandments to adequately answer the question. Or, to put it in His own words: "There is no other [one] commandment greater than these [two]" (Mark 12:31, parentheses mine).

We have learned a simple but profound truth. Man's basic responsibility is twofold—love God and love your neighbor.

Matthew 22:34-40 and Priorities

What does this passage teach us about priorities? I have *two:* God and my neighbor. They are not in sequence. It is not love God for a certain amount of time and to a certain degree and *then* love my neighbor. It is love God *and* love my neighbor. Do them both. Do them both now. Do them both all the time. Christ is saying, "Put God first." He is also saying, "Put your neighbor first." Christ is saying, "Give God top priority." He is also saying, "Give your neighbor top priority."[9]

We need to find another word. *Priority* indicates order and rank; *priority* means one thing is more important than another. Such is not the case. It is not God first and different neighbors second, third, fourth, and so on. It is my responsibility to love God *and at the same time* my responsibility to love my neighbors. Christ is not outlining sequential priorities. He is establishing basic, biblical responsibilities. He is saying, "Here are life's two most important, most significant relationships—God and your neighbor." He is further saying, "Here is your basic responsibility in these two relationships—love."

The Bible emphasizes our significant relationships and our responsibilities in those relationships. The Bible does not present what we traditionally refer to as a "list of priorities." In the remainder of this book we will refer to basic relationships and responsibilities as another way of discussing priorities. Christ is not saying that my responsibility to God is more important than my responsibility to my neighbor.

*B*alance. What a rare trait!

Few things are more important in our topsy-turvy, hurry-up world than balance. The enemy of our souls works overtime to push us toward every imaginable extreme, doesn't he? Few there are who maintain a level-headed mind-set when life's demands increase.

Obviously, balance is one of your desires . . . and I commend you for it. My hope is that this book will help. It is one of those volumes you'll have a hard time putting down.

Please accept my thanks for your contribution to Insight for Living. This book is our way of expressing our gratitude in a tangible manner.

Chuck

He is not saying that my responsibility to my neighbor is less important than my responsibility to God. He is saying that both are important, significant, and divinely-assigned responsibilities.

Matthew 22:34-40 and Self

What does this passage teach us about ourselves? According to Matthew 22:34-40, *I* am also important and significant. I am to love God. I am to love Him with all my heart, soul, and mind. I am to love my neighbor. I am to love that neighbor as I love myself. Thus I need to learn how to love God and how to love my neighbor as myself. I need to fulfill these responsibilities to God, my neighbor, and myself—consistently and effectively. If I am ignorant or inactive, then the responsibilities given to me in Matthew 22:34-40 won't be accomplished. If I am informed and obedient, then those responsibilities will be fulfilled.

That makes me highly important. That means I must assign top priority to my life, my growth, my relationships, my responsibilities. That means everything about me becomes significant—my thoughts, my feelings, my decisions, my body, my attitudes, my sexuality, my words, my reactions.

Yet in the preceding chapters we put ourselves at the bottom of the list! It isn't biblical. If I am going to fulfill my biblical responsibilities to God and my neighbors, I must give myself top priority. Not in place of God. But along with God. Just as my relationship and responsibility to God are of the utmost importance, so my relationship and responsibility to myself are also of the utmost importance. It is not God *then* neighbor *then* self. It is God *and* neighbor *and* self. There is no way we can interpret Matthew 22:34-40 and see ourselves as insignificant. There is no way we can fulfill these two commandments and put ourselves last on a list.

By the Way . . .

There are *three* top priorities in life. My responsibility to God, to others, and to myself. They are closely related to each other. Let's make that a stronger statement. They are inextricably tied together. When you pray, you are loving God. That's putting God first, but it is also putting yourself first, because you benefit from praying. When you memorize Scripture, you are loving God and in so doing putting Him first. At the same time you are profiting from the Word and that means you are meeting your own needs, too. When you worship and praise God, He is pleased because of your response to Him. Those very same activities are also having an impact on your personal growth.

In the same way, when we fulfill a biblical obligation to a neighbor, we put our neighbor first. But the good deed also has numerous positive effects on us. In carrying out our biblical responsibilities to God and neighbors, we are always in some way involved. We are always in some way both contributor and receiver. There is no way we can fulfill the requirement of Matthew 22:34-40 without our personal and strategic involvement.

Chapter Four, Notes

[1]J. Duncan M. Derrett, "Love thy neighbor as a man like thyself"? *Expository Times*, vol. LXXXIII, No. 2 (Nov. 1971), p. 55. "Neighbor" is not just other Jews, for Leviticus 19:17-18, the parable of the Good Samaritan in Luke 10:25-37, and Leviticus 19:34 demonstrate that the Jews were to love their fellow countrymen *and* the stranger or alien in their midst.

[2]Ibid. The phrase "as yourself" would "emphasize both the nearness of the neighbor and the quality of the love."

[3]Victor Paul Furnish, *The Love Command in the New Testament* (Nashville: Abingdon Press, 1972), p. 27. The author has a thorough treatment of both the Matthew and Mark accounts of the Great Commandment, pages 24-34.

[4]Ibid., pp. 26-27.

[5]Ibid., p. 34. "For Matthew . . . these two commandments do not just *contain* or *span* the law, but *constitute* it." David Brown comments: "This is all Scripture in a nutshell; the whole law of human duty in a portable, pocket form. Indeed, it is so *simple* that a child may understand it, so *brief* that all may remember it, so *comprehensive* as to embrace all possible cases." *The Four Gospels: A Commentary, Critical, Experimental and Practical* (London: The Banner of Truth Trust, 1969), p. 189.

[6]Furnish, *The Love Command*, p. 27.

[7]"The point in quoting this commandment in addition to the other is in this instance not the fact that love to God includes love to our neighbor, which is true enough; but that the quality and high character of both commandments are 'alike'." R. C. H. Lenski, *The Interpretation of St. Matthew's Gospel* (Minneapolis: Augsburg Publishing House, 1964), p. 882. In his excellent treatment of self-love, Paul Brownback comments on the intertwining of these two commandments. He writes: "There are some things we can do directly for God. Worship is one, perhaps the only one. But the majority of what we do for God involves loving our neighbor for His sake and to His glory. Therefore, the second commandment is like the first in that it is part and parcel of carrying out the first commandment." *The Danger of Self-Love* (Chicago: Moody Press, 1982), p. 149.

[8]Cf. Samuel J. Schultz, *The Gospel of Moses* (New York: Harper & Row, Publishers, 1974). According to Schultz, these two commandments not only express the essence of the Bible, but also state the minimum requirement for any person who was concerned about life after death (p. ix). He traces these themes through the Old and New Testaments.

[9]Note Galatians 5:14, "For the whole Law is fulfilled in one word, in the statement, 'You shall love your neighbor as yourself.' " Loving God is not mentioned, but it is certainly assumed, for to state one part of the Great Commandment is to assume the whole. Cf. Romans 13:8-9, James 2:8.

CHAPTER FIVE

Singling Out Significant Neighbors

Jan was sitting on the porch of the apartment she shared with three other single working girls. She was mulling over the message she had heard in church that morning on the responsibility of the Christian to love his neighbor. Pastor Franklin had enouraged his congregation to come to the evening's service prepared to ask him questions on the morning message so they could all get a better grasp of the meaning and implications of neighbor-loving.

"Well," said Jan to herself, "the first thing I want to know is which of my many current relationships are really important. Which ones are biblically significant neighbors that I am supposed to love?

"Let's see . . . my three roommates would probably be in this category. And then there's Dad and Mom back home, and my married brother in Toledo . . . and can't forget my current boyfriend, David.

"Who else is there? People at the office. The friends I've made at the racquetball club. Oh yeah, and the guys and gals in the singles group at church.

"I didn't realize that I had so many people in my orbit. I hope the pastor is going to sort out the significant ones and tell us what order to put them in. That's what I need to know right now. I need to get my priorities straight."

Well, Jan—and the rest of you who are wondering about these things—the best way to discover the answers to these questions is to analyze the Scriptures in terms of what they teach about *who* I am to relate to and *how* I am to relate to them. This kind of data will help me identify my biblically significant neighbors and help me ascertain my biblical responsibilities with each of these relationships.

Who Is My Neighbor?

In the last chapter we said my neighbor is that human being who is near or of whom I am aware or both. It is time to explore this. Who are these people? I can't be near everyone. I can't be aware of everyone. So, which relationships are biblically significant? Which neighbors am I obligated to love? This again raises the question of priorities. Is there a hierarchy in these neighbor relationships? Is one neighbor more important than another?

Let's examine Ephesians to find some answers to these questions. Here is a New Testament letter written to new Christians, telling them what they need to know about their position and practice in Christ. If the writer, the apostle Paul, was really on target with truth, wouldn't we expect him to inform the believers at Ephesus about the basics in Matthew 22:34-40: God, self, and others? Could we not also expect him to point out which "others" are really important? And if there is a priority system among these other neighbors, we ought to look carefully to see which one is first, second, third, and so on, according to Paul.

You Are Important

Take a tour of Ephesians looking for truth about yourself. You are blessed, chosen, holy, predestined, adopted, forgiven (1:3-12). That makes you important! You weren't always positioned "in Christ." You used to be dead in sin (2:1-3). Now you are alive and able to glorify God through your life (2:4-10). That makes you important!

You are not alone. Others who are different from you are linked to God along with you. You, individually and corporately, are important (2:11-22). You are members of a new organization—the body of Christ (3:1-12). In that body you are an important, gifted member (4:1-16).

Do you see what the apostle Paul is doing? He is im-

pressing the believer with who he is because of his relationship with God. He is developing, as it were, his spiritual self-
concept. It is important that you know who you are, where you
stand, where you came from, what you have, what you can do,
and who is with you. Paul details that in Ephesians, especially
in chapters 1 through 3. Because of what God has done in your
life, you are important!

We usually say that these three chapters focus on posi-
tional truth. That's right. Whose position? Yours! In God's
program, you are important. Chapters 4 through 6 deal with
practice. Whose practice? Yours! Without you, position and
practice mean nothing. Without God, you have no position. In
Ephesians, as in every book in the Bible, you are important!

Now, About the Church

If we can classify chapters 1 through 3 as being intensely *intra*personal, then we can say that chapters 4 through
6 are intensely *inter*personal, for Paul now relates you to your
significant neighbors. First, he talks about your walk with
other believers—other members of the body—the church. He
makes it patently clear that your relationships with other believers are exceedingly important. He spells out in chapter 4
some of the basic responsibilities that every believer has to
other believers. "Speaking the truth in love," for example, is
one of these responsibilities (4:15, 25). He does not say do this
after you love God and *after* you love your family. He says do it.
Every one of you. Right now.

Does this mean that because Paul refers to relationships in the church first, that he is assigning the church top
priority among the significant others in our lives? Hardly. It
means that Paul keeps up a logical train of thought. He talks
about the believer's position in the body in chapter 3 and goes
on to talk about the believer's practice in the body in chapter 4.
He says nothing about the church having priority over other
relationships. Nor does he say anything about other relationships having priority over the church. We keep looking for
"what is more important than what." Paul is very careful not to
tell us. He is not thinking about sequential priorities. He is
thinking about basic relationships. The church is one of
those.

Now, About the Family

Stimulated by the concepts of love (5:2) and submission (5:21), Paul next heads for home with the truth. Believers are not assembled for study and fellowship all of the time. After church is over, you usually go home. Therein lies another whole set of biblically significant relationships and responsibilities, says Paul.

First, he writes a word to wives about submission (5:22-24), then a word to husbands about love (5:25-33). Next he writes to children about obedience and respect (6:1-3), and finally, to fathers about discipline and instruction (6:4). In a few short verses Paul places certain basic responsibilities upon those in marriage and family relationships. He sets up no priorities. Paul doesn't say do these things first and then work on church duties. He indicates that, along with obligations in the context of the church there are obligations that are *just as important* in marriage and family living. He doesn't exhort couples to work on their marriages first and then address themselves to child rearing. Both are important. Work on both of them. He doesn't say to the husband that his responsibility to love his wife is more important than his responsibility to love other members of the body. He indicates that God demands both. Nor does he tell a wife she is under a primary obligation to submit to her husband and only secondarily should she concern herself about using her spiritual gift in the body. He is simply saying that basic obligations are placed upon all the family members. Do them.

Now, About the Job

Church and home. Two basic, biblical relationships, each meriting top priority. When you are not in church or not at home, where are you? At work—on the job. You are either in a management role (master) or an employee role (slave). If you are an employee, you are to render your services obediently and genuinely (6:5-8). If you are an employer, you are to treat those who work for you kindly and impartially (6:9).

Employer/employee—another set of basic, biblical relationships that carry with them certain God-given responsibilities. Again Paul assigns no priority. He does not say that after you fulfill your obligations in the church and in the home, *then* you should work on doing God's will on the job. He gives no indication that it is more important for you to serve God rightly in the church than it is to serve rightly in your work. Both are equally important.

Paul is not developing a list, he is identifying categories. If we said to Paul, "Now that you have commented on responsibilities in the church, home, and job, please tell us which one takes priority over the other. We want to make sure our priorities are straight." Paul would probably stare at us blankly and respond, "I don't think I follow you. What do you mean 'which one takes priority?' "

"Well, we are busy people and we don't always have the time to do everything, so if we have to ease up on one of these, which one should it be? In other words, which one of these relationships and which of these responsibilities is God *really* concerned about?"

"All of them. Each and every one of them. They are all significant relationships. They all have things that must be done. They all require obedience. Or, to put it in your words, they all take priority."

Now, About the World

There is still another basic neighbor category. Paul addresses it in Ephesians 6:10-20. It is the satanically-controlled world in which we live. That is why he says, "Put on the full armor of God, that you may be able to stand firm against the schemes of the devil" (6:11). He then outlines what it takes for the believer to "stand firm" against this unbelieving, corrupt world system.

Actually, Paul has already introduced this area of life in 5:3-14, where, among other things, we are instructed not to participate "in the unfruitful deeds of darkness, but instead even expose them" (5:11). The world system is not off in some corner. It invades our churches, our homes, our work situations, and we must relate to it in those contexts. But it is broader than that. It impacts our society, our culture, our educational systems, our political systems, our media systems. Our assignment: to separate ourselves from it, yet at the same time to minister to it. Our responsibilities and resources are detailed in 6:10-20.

Now, let's not miss the overall point. I am to have a certain kind of relationship with this devil-dominated world system. Paul mentions it last, but certainly not because it is least. It is another one of my basic, biblical relationships. This is where a basic responsibility to witness comes in. In a parallel passage in Colossians (4:2-6), Paul comments specifically on this evangelistic ministry to outsiders.

Again, note that Paul assigns no high or low priority to this area. He doesn't tell us to take care of the church and the home and the job and *then* deal with the world system. Witnessing is also a top level obligation, just as important as the other areas we have discussed. Paul doesn't say edify the body, *then* witness. He doesn't say love your wife, *then* witness. He doesn't say honor your parents, *then* witness. Don't you see the logical fallacy in this sequential approach? If you wait till the body is edified totally, then you'll never witness. If you wait till you have loved your wife enough, then you'll never witness. If you wait till you have fully honored your parents, you'll never get to witness. Along with all of our other responsibilities, we believers are to impact our world.

Now, About Government

There is one other significant neighbor category. Paul doesn't refer to it in Ephesians, but he does in Romans. Note how Romans 1-8 is similar to Ephesians 1-3 in that it deals with the individual before and after salvation. If believers are going to adequately carry out their responsibilities to love God and love neighbor, they need to understand all that is true of them, and then think, feel, and act on that basis. Romans 9-11 addresses the same issues with regard to the Jews. In chapter 12, Paul presents responsibilities with regard to one set of significant neighbors—the church.

Chapter 13 introduces another significant neighbor category—civil government. Paul here sets forth the believer's prime responsibilities to submit and to support his government (13:1-7). These are not options. Body responsibilities don't take precedence over them. Since every believer is a citizen of some country, every believer has this relationship and these obligations. They don't come *after* anything. It is just as important for a believer to pay his taxes as it is for him to give to his church. It is just as important for a Christian to vote intelligently in the primary elections as it is for her to study her Sunday school lesson or to build a good relationship with her husband. Civil government is ordained by God, as is the individual, the family, the church, work, and the world. The responsibilities of good citizenship are incumbent on every Christian.

Now, in Conclusion

God's Word, in germinal form in Matthew 22, establishes three basic relationships—God, self, and neighbor. Other portions of Scripture (for example, Ephesians and Romans[1]), elaborate clearly who these biblically significant neighbors are and what we are to do with them, to them, and for them. So now we have God, self, church, family, work, government, and world as our basic, biblical relationships.

These relationships and the responsibilities therein are obviously quite different. My responsibilities to my wife are not the same as my responsibilities to my employer. But different as they may be, each of them is a God-imposed obligation. Scripture doesn't say, "Here are some things you must do with regard to your wife, and here are some things it would be nice if you could find time to do with regard to your employer." Scripture doesn't say, "Here is a level one relationship: give it so much time and energy. Here is a level two relationship: you can give it less attention. And here is level three: do what you can with it." The Bible simply does not present the Christian's commitments on some scale or list. It does not give them to us as sequential responsibilities; it presents them as simultaneous responsibilities. We don't do them all at the same time (though there are many areas of overlap), but we need to do them all.

By the Way . . .

At this point you may be talking to yourself about schedules and calendars and "things to do" lists, all of which demand a priority assignment. You're right. In a given time period, say, for example, a day or a week, we should—and do—assign priority to certain relationships and responsibilities. We do this to remind ourselves to get certain things done, to be more efficient in the use of our time and energy, to take care of things we have been neglecting, to meet some specific needs that have arisen.

All day yesterday I worked in the yard, the garage, and the shop—mowing, weeding, watering, cleaning, repairing, building. Some weeks I do a bit of that each evening; some weeks I do it all on Saturday. My responsibility is to get it done regularly. If I spend all my spare time doing these tasks, then I will neglect some other biblical responsibilities. If I never mow, trim, and weed I'm neglecting another set of biblical responsibilities. My job is to keep my total life in biblical balance: to make sure that I am fulfilling all my biblical obligations. Daily schedules and weekly calendars facilitate this. Schedules and calendars will change. The Word of God won't.

Chapter Five, Notes

[1] Paul follows a similar pattern in Colossians, dealing with a number of the believer's significant relationships. Peter does the same thing in his first letter. The Corinthian letters address themselves to certain questions and problems; nevertheless, as one reads them one is impressed with the references to church matters, marriage issues, Satan and the world system, legal matters, and other basic areas of relationships and responsibilities. Actually, all of the New Testament letters can be analyzed profitably in this way.

CHAPTER SIX

Circles of Priorities

By now I hope I have you thinking more deeply about the traditional approach to priorities. More specifically, I trust you are questioning the first—second—third approach. Many speakers and writers are giving out their numbered lists. Not many of them, however, clearly explain how to live "by the numbers," because it is a concept that defies a logical, rational, livable explanation. I have tried to demonstrate this fact in previous chapters by posing a lot of bewildering questions that arise out of this system, and by suggesting some of the absurd conclusions one can draw from the same system.

I would like to suggest that we scrap the list of priorities and adopt in its place circles of relationships and responsibilities. This approach will enable us to develop a system that is practical, biblical, and explainable.

Where Does God Go?

Instead of talking about putting God first in life, let's talk about putting God at the center of life—making God central to everything. So we start with this:

Where Does Self Go?

What do we do with self? This is the question that plagues every designer of priority lists. We need to show self in relation to God. Here is one way to graphically do this:

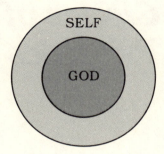

The first thing that this shows is that the individual is a Christian. For the non-Christian, someone or something else is at the core of his or her life. It may be another person, a religion, a possession, or an ambition. But it isn't God. A Christian is related to God, and we show this by placing God in the inner circle. This demonstrates not only the reality of God in the believer's life, but the centrality of God in that life. It is one way of capturing the essence of Matthew 22:37: "You shall love the Lord your God with all your heart, and with all your soul, and with all your mind."

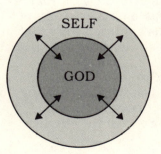

The concentric circles highlight the fact that if and when God is at the center of my life, He can potentially touch each and every area of me as a person. The arrows demonstrate that God and I are relating to each other in various ways. Note that the arrows go in both directions. I study His Word; He renews my mind. I come to grips with His holiness; He changes my thought life. I learn about Him as my creator and redeemer; He applies those truths to my physical body. As this process takes place I am putting God first in my life, giving Him first priority. At the same time, because of these same transactions *I am putting myself first.* I am learning, growing, and changing. I am fulfilling my biblical responsibilities to God and to myself.

Let's place ourselves, for a moment, on the second floor of Parker Hall, a women's dorm at the state university. The room at the end of the hall is occupied by Carla, the floor RA. Carla is a Christian and right now she is praying. She could be studying, resting, fixing her hair, talking on the phone, or listening to the radio, but right now she is praying. God tells us to pray, and when we do we are obeying Him and He is pleased. Prayer is one specific thing Carla can do to put God first in her life.

But Carla is not a mindless robot in this process. When she prays, *things are happening to her.* She is learning to discipline herself to carve time out of her busy schedule to talk with God. She is learning how to concentrate, because it is easy for her mind to wander to other things while she is praying. She is learning to articulate her fears, frustrations, and heartaches. She is learning to believe that though she can't see God, He is there, He is listening, He will answer. Certainly prayer is putting God first, but anytime I do anything to put God first, I profit, I benefit, I learn, I grow. Do you see it? When God is central in my life, He can become *significant* in every aspect of my person. When God is central in my life, I can relate and respond to every aspect of His person.

What About Others?

What do we do with family, church, work, world, and government? We can add them to our diagram in the following way.

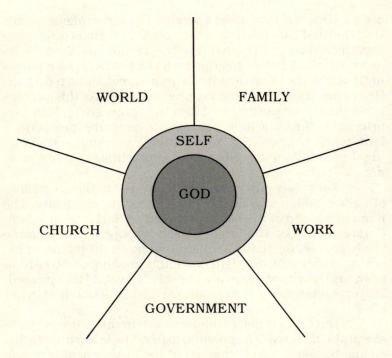

This takes priorities off a list and wraps them around a life! Note that there is no order, no hierarchy, and no numbering among the five significant neighbor categories. Each segment is the same size, showing that each is an equally important God-given area of responsibility. The particular segment designations are arbitrary. They could be switched around and it would make no difference. There is no right way to read this, i.e., clockwise or counterclockwise. The fact that "church" is placed between "government" and "world" is arbitrary. Any category could be placed next to any other category. This fits in beautifully with Paul's approach in Ephesians and Romans. He mentions a given category, develops it briefly, and goes on to another. He never indicates that he is ranking them according to a certain scale or organizing them in a particular format. His point: All five are important. And that is the point of the diagram.

What About Overlapping?

One of the weaknesses of this diagram is that it doesn't show overlapping and interrelationships between these various categories. They appear as separate, isolated items. But this is not the case in life. For example, suppose Bob hears a sermon in church on Ephesians 5:11, challenging him to be willing to expose the unfruitful works of darkness. The next week he reads in the newspaper that his state legislature is considering a bill to lower the drinking age to sixteen. Bob responds by expressing his concerns in a letter to the editor of the local newspaper and one to his state senator. See what has happened? In one life situation, there are interlocking relationships involving Bob, God, the church, the world, and government.

To Whom Am I Related?

There is another important feature in this diagram. It portrays clearly that I as an individual have a relationship with each of the five significant others. Note how the "self circle" touches every neighbor relationship on the diagram. The nature of each relationship does change, but the fact of each relationship does not. Each relationship is permanent, yet each is dynamic. Take work, for instance. You start as an apprentice, then move to journeyman, and on up the ladder. For a while you are in production; then you transfer to marketing. You start out making a little; you end up (maybe) making a lot of money. You work for yourself; then you work for someone else. Eventually you may retire. A lot of different circumstances, but all through this scenario, you have been relating to your work.

We relate to Democrats in office, then to Republicans. We listen to honest politicians and to the other kind. We remain single for awhile; then maybe we fall in love and get married and step into a whole new set of family relationships. We get a new pastor, we build a new church building, we serve on a new committee, yet it is all in the context of the church. In the world we have to relate to the never-ending, ever-changing beauty of creation *and* to the ever-present ugliness of sin. We have learned to relate to computers, we're learning to relate to word processors, and now it looks like we are going to have to learn to relate with robots! It's all part of the world we live in.

What Can I Leave Out?

The relationships you have to each of the significant neighbor categories are not optional. They are obligations. You can't say, "I'm tired of being a citizen. For the next year I'm going to block out that relationship and its responsibilities as nonexistent for me." You can't do that. As long as you are alive and residing in this nation, you are a citizen with biblical responsibilities. You can't say, "I'll relate to my elderly parents when I have the time." You have to take time. It's an obligation. You can't say, "When I get settled in my new job, then I'll meet my mate's needs." You can't preempt family responsibilities like that. You have an obligation to your job *and* to your mate. Every one of these neighbor relationships is biblical; therefore, every one of them is mandatory. You don't have the option of "trying to get to it someday when you have the time."

How Does God Work in and through Me?

Notice something else in this diagram. As God works with me, He wants to do something *in* me and *through* me. He wants me to become an informed, obedient child of God. He wants me to become someone whose entire being is growing and developing more and more into Christlikeness. That is God at work in me. But I don't exist in isolation. I live in the context of these five neighbor relationships, and God wants to work through me to impact each of these areas.

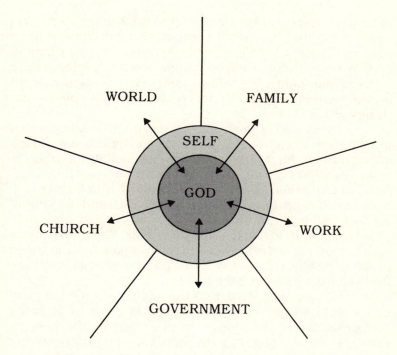

As I experience personal growth this should affect interpersonal growth. For example, my mind should be renewed as a result of studying and meditating on the Word of God. As this process is taking place I should use this renewed mind to analyze the needs of my wife, to respond to my disobedient child, to interact with the boss's orders, to inform my foot that the speed limit is 55 mph, to decide how to vote on the issue coming up at the next church business meeting, to evaluate the evening news on television, and to cope with the various sale items in the new catalog.

I need to level with you about catalogs. I am a tool addict. I'm strongly influenced by "30% off" deals. Easily manipulated by the "buy two and get a lower price" teaser. Highly motivated by the "sale ends the 29th" deadline. Another Sears Sale Catalog has arrived. I rip off the wrapper and go for the tool section. The pictures, printing, and prices soon convince me that without these tools I can do nothing! Not that sale catalogs are all bad, but the world system can get to me through them, persuading me that the most important thing in life is a band saw, and I'll not be fulfilled until I get mine. But my personal growth should enable me to handle my coveting and their catalogs. It is happening—slowly. And as it does happen, I find myself better able to teach my children how to not love the things of this world.

That's God at work in me and through me, impacting my significant neighbor relationships and motivating and enabling me to fulfill my basic, biblical responsibilities. I can try to do this all on my own, using human wisdom and human effort, but that would leave God out. His desire is that He be central in my life and therefore *significant* in each and every one of my basic, biblical relationships.

Again the arrows go both directions. That is to help me realize that not only do God's truth and power equip me to function rightly in these five areas, but the experiences I have in these areas drive me back to God.

For example, Barbara is the mother of a teething toddler who is not yet toilet trained and is given to throwing temper tantrums. How does all of this behavior affect her? It drives her right straight up the wall! It also ought to drive her back to God. From Him she can learn patience and persistence—two qualities needed by all mothers. And fathers. Children have a way of stimulating parents to enroll in God's continuing education program.

In a similar vein, Supreme Court decisions on abortion revive our interest in the ethical teaching of the Word of God. Gossip conveyed on the church's "care and share" network forces us to think carefully about God's concept of truth. The arrival in today's mail of another credit card may prompt some thinking about money, credit, contentment, and covetousness—issues about which God has something to say.

What Have We Got?

What have we accomplished with our approach? We have established a new way of looking at life. Rather than trying to live by a list, it's better to go around in circles! You might call them "circles of priorities." If you do, recognize that every label on the diagram represents a number one priority. Remember also that at the heart of this model is the truth stated in Matthew 22:34-40: Love God and love your neighbor. This approach is simply another (and, I trust, better) way of integrating these basic relationships and responsibilities into a more cohesive and coherent process.

By the Way . . .

This model is not a *time* chart. The five neighbor segments do not represent equal blocks of time. It takes time to fulfill these obligations, but the diagram doesn't speak to that issue. We will discuss the time aspect later.

Nor is this a *truth* chart. The five neighbor segments do not tell us that each area has the same amount and kind of biblical truth to be applied. Some responsibilities are common to all five areas. But in each area God has also given us truth that is uniquely pertinent to that particular relationship. In the model, the five areas are equal in size and shape to show that each one has biblical significance and biblical obligations. But these areas are not identical.

This is not the only way to categorize significant others, but we have demonstrated that it is a biblical way. These five categories provide a completeness of essentials, though not a comprehensiveness of details. We will work on these details in the following chapters. (One might ask where you would put enemies. It depends on who they are—an in-law, a section foreman, a city council member. . . !)

If this approach to priorities looks easier, don't believe it. It's tougher to live this way than to live by a list. In this approach God tells me what is important and imperative. In a priority list someone else with less authority is scaling down my responsibilities.

CHAPTER SEVEN

How to Love

Recall the confrontation we described in chapter 4 between the Pharisee and Christ. In that conversation Jesus made it clear that man's basic responsibility is to love—to love God and to love his neighbor. Now that we have established how to relate God, self, and neighbor to each other and who our significant neighbors are, it is imperative that we explore the meaning of love.

How to Love God

How do you love God? Very simple. Keep His commandments. The apostle John put it very clearly. "For this is the love of God, that we keep His commandments; and His commandments are not burdensome" (1 John 5:3). God the Son repeated this concept a number of times to his disciples. "If you love Me, you will keep My commandments" (John 14:15). "He who has My commandments and keeps them, he it is who loves Me" (John 14:21). The Old Testament injunction to "love the LORD your God with all your heart and with all your soul and with all your might" is preceded and followed by specific things Israel was to do to demonstrate this love (Deuteronomy 6:1-15). Elsewhere (Deuteronomy 13:1-4), Moses told Israel that God would test their love of Him by seeing how they responded to a false prophet. If they succumbed, their love was fickle. To demonstrate a genuine love for God, said Moses, "You shall follow the LORD your God and fear Him;

and you shall keep His commandments, listen to His voice, serve Him, and cling to Him" (Deuteronomy 13:4).

You love God by keeping His commandments. That lifts love out of the realm of pious thoughts and warm, fuzzy feelings about our heavenly Father. Love is knowing what He expects us to do, and doing it.

Things are quite similar in the human family. Audrey and I have four children. They love us, and through the years they have each expressed their love in a variety of ways—handmade birthday cards, a craft, a bouquet of flowers, a picture, a gift, or just spontaneous, unsolicited words of love and appreciation. But I'll tell you something that gives us even more intense satisfaction: *when they do what we tell them to do!* And believe me, it puts a lot of static in the system when they say they love us and they don't obey us. We want both affection and obedience from our kids, but if for some reason we were forced to choose between the two, we would opt for obedience. In the final analysis, cold obedience is to be preferred over warm rebellion. As a heavenly Father, God also wants both affection and obedience from His children. But He will not allow us to substitute nebulous sentiment for informed obedience.

"You shall have no other gods before Me" (Exodus 20:3). This is one of His commandments. It deals with my relationship to Him. "I say to every man among you not to think more highly of himself than he ought to think; but to think so as to have sound judgment" (Romans 12:3). This is another one of his commandments. It deals with my relationship to myself. "Conduct yourselves with wisdom toward outsiders" (Colossians 4:5). This is yet another one of His commandments. It deals with my relationship to the non-Christian. Is there a priority structure among these three commandments? Not at all. I am to do all three of them, because they are all His commandments. And if I love Him, I will keep all of His commandments. Thus to love God is to relate properly to Him, to my neighbor, and to myself. Guess what? We are right back in Matthew 22. The Lord knew what He was talking about. The two commandments are inextricably related to each other. We love God by keeping His commandments. In so doing, we will rightly relate to ourselves and others.

How to Love Your Neighbor

How do you love your neighbor? Very simple. Keep the commandments that have to do with your biblically significant neighbors. Provide for your family (1 Timothy 5:8), contribute to the needs of the saints (Romans 12:13), subject yourself to the governing authorities (Romans 13:1), be just and fair with your employees (Colossians 4:1), resist the devil (James 4:7), and on and on the list goes. You love your neighbor by discovering your biblically significant responsibilities in these relationships and doing them.

Let's assume that you are a Christian and that a non-Christian comes into your life. It may be the new bus driver, the paperboy, a fellow employee, a new in-law. At any rate, this person now becomes a biblically significant neighbor to you. Your biblical responsibility is to be an ambassador from God to that person, creatively and consistently giving him or her the word of reconciliation (2 Corinthians 5:18-21). You carry on this witness by the way you act and the way you speak (Colossians 4:5-6). That's the way you love your unsaved neighbor.

As with loving God, loving your neighbor is not just having some kind of nice, pleasant feeling toward others. It involves a full range of attitudes and actions. Furthermore, when you are discharging these neighbor responsibilities, you aren't neglecting God—you are obeying Him.

There is another side to loving your neighbor. The side we have been looking at has a highly *propositional* orientation; that is, the commandments state in propositional form how we are to think, feel, and act with regard to our neighbors. The other side of the coin presents loving your neighbor in a highly *personal* orientation. For example, the Lord told the story of the Good Samaritan to impress upon his listeners two things. First, your neighbor is that person who has a need that you are aware of and can meet. Second, you love that neighbor by acting to meet his need (Luke 10:25-37). Propositionally stated, this would be "do good to all men" (Galatians 6:10), but in Luke 10 the thrust is personal—look at the person, determine his need, and act to meet that need.

In 1 John 4:10, John gives a classic definition of love that has this personal orientation. He starts out with his typical introductory formula, "in this," a formula he often uses to alert his readers that a clear, concise definition will follow.[1] The concept he is going to define is *agape*—God's love. "Not that we loved God, but that He loved us" indicates that God's love is not a reciprocating but an initiating love. It originates with the lover. "And sent His Son" emphasizes the fact that God's love acts; it doesn't just feel—it does something. We must also add that this action of sending His Son away from Him to suffer and die could be classified as no less than a sacrificial action. *Agape* is willing to give—to give in, to give up.

The lover—God—focuses on the need of the ones being loved. Our basic need is to have our sins forgiven and to be given a righteousness acceptable to God. He sent His Son to meet that need in our lives, "to be the propitiation [satisfaction] for our sins." Remember the ingredients of love in Luke 10—look at the person, determine his need, and act to meet that need. The original pattern is given in 1 John 4:10. God looked at us, determined our need, and initiated a sacrificial action to meet that need.

Now let's move to verse 11. "Beloved, if God so [in this manner] loved us, we also [in the same manner] ought to love one another." If we have experienced the love spoken of in verse 10, we are obligated by verse 11 to express it to others. How do you love your neighbor? By taking the initiative and acting sacrificially to meet his needs.[2]

What is the difference between the propositional and the personal approach to loving your neighbor? In the final analysis, nothing. For when I am obeying God's commandments with regard to my neighbor, I will be acting properly to meet the legitimate needs of my neighbor. What does a disobedient child need? Discipline. When I act to meet that need, I am functioning in harmony with the Word of God. For example, Proverbs 22:15 states: "Foolishness is bound up in the heart of a child; the rod of discipline will remove it far from him."

If the same child is in the store begging for another toy when he already has plenty of things to play with, and I buy it for him, that isn't real love. That would be acting improperly to meet illegitimate needs. Scripture helps me know what needs are legitimate and what actions are proper to meet them. What does an unsaved person need? The gospel. When I act to meet that need I am putting the truth of Acts 1:8 into effect. Obeying the commandments and acting to meet needs are mutually inclusive concepts.

How to Love Yourself

How do we love ourselves? Very simple. If love is keeping the commandments, then we love ourselves by keeping those commandments which relate specifically to us as individuals. In so doing we will be acting properly to meet our legitimate needs.

Meet my friend Harold. He is thirty-five years old and an extremely successful computer salesman. He is handsome, intelligent, and articulate. He and Shirley have been married for eight years and have two small daughters. About three months ago Harold became a Christian. The message he got from some other Christians was that for thirty-five years he had engaged in self-love, and now he was to stop that and start loving God and others. Harold was to regard himself as nothing, so God could be everything. Harold got the impression that it would be best if he would just sort of fade into the woodwork; that God's desire was to "put Harold down."

One Sunday morning his pastor spoke on Romans 12:1-3. The message was entitled: "What Is Best for You." His opening words captured Harold's attention:

> How do you love your children?
> By doing what's best for them.
> Then how would you love yourself?
> The same way. By doing what's best for you.
> How do you find out what's best for you?
> Read the Word of God.
> Then how do you love yourself?
> By doing what the Word of God says.
> Let's look at Romans 12:1-3. It tells us how to
>   love ourselves, because it tells us what we
>   can do that is best for us.

And then the pastor proceeded to show from these three verses that the best thing you can do for yourself is to present yourself to God; not conform yourself to this world; let yourself be transformed; renew your mind; determine the will of God for yourself; and accurately appraise your giftedness.

Harold went away from that service enlightened and challenged. He mulled things over all afternoon.

God must know that I need a worthy cause, a person to follow, a master to serve, and so He commands me to present myself unreservedly to Him. Well, if that's what I need, then that's what I am going to do. I am going to act to meet that need in my life right now.

And right there in his easy chair in the family room, Harold told the Lord he was making himself available for whatever God wanted to do with him. It was the best thing he had ever done for himself. Or to put it in other words, it was a proper act of self-love on Harold's part.

Being the aggressive, ambitious type, Harold figured that he might as well stick with the best. In the weeks that followed, he moved into verse two and began to act to meet more of his legitimate needs. He realized that his ideas on money were well-conformed to the world's perspective, and he set out to make changes where changes were needed. He started cutting back in voluntary overtime, started spending more time with Shirley and the kids, started giving more money to his church, stopped worrying about whether he was in line for promotion to sales manager, and began to be more precise with his expense account. These changes didn't come easily or automatically. When the pressures to remain conformed to the world came, Harold would smile and say to himself, "Look, old buddy, I'm only doing what's best for you, and the reason I'm doing what's best for you is . . . because I love you!"

Harold began to realize that to live the Christian life he did need to "put sin down" but he didn't need to "put himself down." Each time he engaged in doing what God wanted him to do, he was, in effect, loving God. At the same time he was loving himself, because he was acting properly to meet his own legitimate needs.

The Bible is full of truths we are to apply to ourselves, as Harold did with Romans 12:1-3. How about Philippians 4:6-7? When I am anxious, I need to talk to someone. God says, "talk to Me in prayer," and to obey that exhortation is to love God. But the very same act of praying meets my needs, for when I obey the commandment of verse 6, I learn how to pray and I receive the promise of verse 7—peace.

In the act of loving God, I am also loving myself, because the very act He commands works to meet my needs. To develop a priority list with God at the top and self at the bottom is to fail to perceive the integrated nature of obedience. When I obey God, He is glorified and I am benefited. The psalmist said, "In Thy presence is fulness of joy" (Psalm 16:11). To be in His presence is to walk in fellowship with Him—to put Him first. But when I do that, what happens? Do I go to the bottom of some list? Do I fade out of the picture? No, my emotions become top priority with God and He gives me fulness of joy. I cannot love God without reaping personal benefits. By the same token, I cannot disobey God without eventually experiencing adverse effects.

Loving yourself is not some frothy sentiment. Nor is it an egotistical self-centeredness. It is obedience: obedience to the commandments of God that have to do with self. There are many of them. We'll explore them in the next chapter.

By the Way . . .

If loving my neighbor involves acting properly to meet his legitimate needs, and loving myself involves acting properly to meet my legitimate needs, would it be valid to say that loving God involves acting properly to meet His legitimate needs?

"Wait a minute," comes a quick reply. "God doesn't have any needs."

"Are you sure about that?"

"Sure I'm sure. God is perfect and perfection would exclude needs."

"Oh, I see what you're saying. Only imperfect people have needs. Our human needs came into being after the fall. Before the fall Adam and Eve didn't have any needs. They didn't need each other. They didn't need to eat. They didn't need to sleep. They didn't need to work. They didn't need to fellowship with their Creator. Only finite, fallen people have needs. Is that what you are saying?"

"Well, I thought that's what I was saying. But now, I'm not so sure. You have stimulated my thinking. If perfect creatures have needs, then a perfect Creator may have needs too. I never thought about that before."

It's a thought worth exploring. But we haven't time to do it now. So read on![3]

Chapter Seven, Notes

[1]Cf. 1 John 2:3, 5; 3:10, 16; 4:2, 9, 13; 5:2.

[2]These factors can be seen in 1 John 3:16-18, Titus 3:4, and in Philippians where the love commended in 1:9 is a love that acted to meet Paul's needs as detailed in 4:10-19.

[3]Human beings have needs, not only because they are fallen, but also because they are finite. If we weren't fallen we would still have needs. God is neither fallen nor finite, so He does not have needs in the same sense that we do, but He is a *person*, and as such has those needs inherent in a *divine person*. All those needs are met completely and perfectly in the Trinity (for example, the need to love and be loved). As a divine Father He desires that His children love, serve, worship, and obey Him. When we fail to do these things, God is not incomplete as a person, but He is disappointed and grieves over our failure. God wants to be our happy heavenly Father. Our obedience meets that desire.

PART 3

Examining Relationships and Responsibilities

CHAPTER EIGHT

You and God

Status quo. It seems like many Christians are barely able to maintain it. (Incidently, *status quo* is a Latin phrase which has been freely translated into English as "the mess we are in"!) Christians were not only born to live, they were born to grow. This whole book is on growth, but this particular chapter will probe what it means to grow in your relationship with God.

Growth involves expansion and change. Expansion of knowledge. Change of behavior. To avoid becoming static and fixed, and following a "no-growth" policy, my knowledge of God and myself should be expanding, and my whole life should be changing. Growth needs to be a dynamic process.

Expanding Our Knowledge of God

The first thing we need to do to expand our knowledge of God is to enlarge the inner circle and identify some truths about God we need to know and act upon.

All the words that appear in the inner circle of our diagram are qualities and characteristics of God. To develop a relationship with Him we must know the meaning and implications of each for our lives. I need truth. His Word contains it. I need the ability to understand the truth. His Spirit will teach me. I need strength to cope with inner turmoil. He is omnipotent. I need a model to follow. Christ is God in human form. I need standards. He is righteous. I need acceptance. He is love. I need to know who is in charge. He is.

The items in the inner circle are representative, not exhaustive. There is no priority assignment. One attribute is not more important than another. One member of the Trinity is not more significant than another. We grow as we interact with each and every one of these concepts.

Our responsibility is to grapple with *all* that is true of God. That is why Paul told the Ephesians that "I did not shrink from declaring to you anything that was profitable. . . . declaring to you the whole purpose of God" (Acts 20:20, 27). Later he wrote to the same people, exhorting them to "be imitators of God" (Ephesians 5:1), and to "put on the full armor of God" (Ephesians 6:11). His own philosophy of life substantiated this, for he wanted to "know Him" (Philippians 3:10) because "in Him all the fulness of Deity dwells in bodily form" (Colossians 2:9). Peter climaxed his second letter by telling his readers that the only way to keep from going astray was to "grow in the grace and knowledge of our Lord and Savior Jesus Christ" (2 Peter 3:17-18).

J. I. Packer says that we have "conformed to the modern spirit: the spirit, that is, that spawns great thoughts of man and leaves room for only small thoughts of God." We have "allowed God to become remote."[1] Christians who don't have an expanding, deepening knowledge of God are like players who have no coach, no rule book, no game schedule, no playing field, no training program. They are depending on one thing—uniforms.

David, in Psalm 139, demonstrates that he knows God, that he has come to grips with the nature of God, and that he has related certain attributes of God to his own human experience. In verses 1 through 6 he brings the omniscience of God to bear on the most complex and confusing life he is aware of—his own. "O LORD, Thou hast searched me and known me" (139:1). In verses 7 through 12, he welds the omnipresence of God to his own elusiveness. "Where can I go from Thy Spirit? Or where can I flee from Thy presence?" (139:7). In verses 13 through 16 he links the omnipotence of God to the most intricate and intriguing being he has ever met—himself. "For Thou didst form my inward parts; Thou didst weave me in my mother's womb" (139:13). In verses 19 through 24, he confronts the sin of man with the holiness and justice of God, and becomes so personally involved that he says, "Do I not hate those who hate Thee, O LORD?" (139:21). In the final verses he internalizes this even more when he requests the holy God to search his own heart (139:23-24). Here was a man who put

God first. Not because he put God at the top of some priority list, but because he was fulfilling his responsibility *to God and to himself* to be more intimately acquainted with his Creator and Redeemer.

We are to love God. That involves keeping His commandments. He commands us to know Him. Knowing God is a life-long task that should have strategic importance for every believer. And as we get to know Him we are acting to meet our own needs. *We need to know Him.* Consistent interaction with the person and work of God is one of the Christian's basic responsibilities. It is a top priority.

Expanding Our Knowledge of Ourselves

The you that is going to grow is an amazing combination of body, soul, and spirit—material and immaterial. Using our circular model, let's expand the "self circle" and begin to indicate areas that need to be understood and brought into conformity with the will of God.

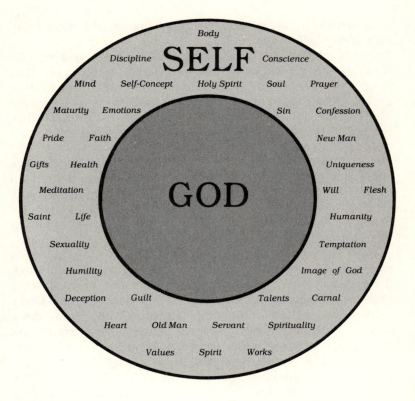

We need to ask some questions. Which of these areas of self is the most important? Which takes priority? Which one can I put off for a few months? Which ones are optional? Which ones are only for the super-committed? You already know the answer. Each and every one of them is important. I need to understand what God's Word teaches about each area, I need to discern how these truths apply to me, and I need to obey.

Granted, I can't do this all at once, but if healthy, wholistic growth is taking place in me, it will involve—over given time periods—attention to each of the areas in the larger circle above. My goal is that of entire sanctification (1 Thessalonians 5:23) and total Christlikeness (Galatians 4:19). Thus, all of my personal endowments are to be presented as instruments of righteousness (Romans 6:13); my body and every asset within it is to be progressively transformed into a more holy lifestyle (Romans 12:1-2).

Granted, also, that some areas are basic and foundational to others. Knowing is foundational to doing, but that doesn't mean knowing is more important than doing. James makes it clear that both are important and both are inseparable (1:22-25, 4:17). A knowledge of the death of Christ (Romans 6) is basic to an understanding of the Christian life (Romans 8), but both are equally important.

Granted, furthermore, that each responsibility takes time. I am to pray without ceasing (1 Thessalonians 5:17), I am to use my spiritual gift (1 Timothy 4:14), and I am to diligently study the Word (2 Timothy 2:15). Each of these could take all of my time. I am responsible to see that I do all three, and must allot my time accordingly.

The items listed in the "self" circle are one person's selection. They could be restated in different terms, combined, divided, added to. The point is that God wants to work in my total person and my total person is extremely complex. God's commandments relate generally or specifically to all these areas; I have needs in all these areas; I must grow—expand and change—in all these areas. To obey God and properly love myself is to know and do God's will in each facet of my life. This means I must give myself top priority.

There are many resources currently available to help the Christian expand his awareness and change his behavior in various facets of his life. Consequently, I am not going to develop each and every one of these topics. Instead, I would like to select two areas and show how they might be treated.

Discernment

The process of living the Christian life involves believing, understanding, discerning, and doing. At least these are four words that Scripture uses to describe the process. Obviously, there are lots of other words, but what I want to do is single out the concept of *discerning.*

Discerning stands midway between understanding and doing. I am to relate what I *know* (understand) to a given life situation and discern what I should *do.* For example, the purpose of the renewing of the mind in Romans 12:2 is to *prove* what the will of God is. Prove means to test, to investigate, to figure things out, to think things through.[2] Knowing the facts is important, but facts alone are sterile. I must take the facts out of my mental locker and use them—testing to determine if and how they apply in a certain situation. On the basis of this discerning process I decide to engage in the action which is in harmony with the will of God.

Our "discerner" must always be turned on and tuned in, for each life situation has its unique features. Thus, Paul instructs the Thessalonians to "examine everything carefully; hold fast to that which is good; abstain from every form of evil (1 Thessalonians 5:21-22). Maturity, says the writer of Hebrews, comes as a result of having one's perceptive capacities highly trained to "discern good and evil" (5:14).[3]

"Hi," I said to the fellow putting on his topcoat a few feet away from me. We were both getting ready to leave the church after attending a wedding. He stared right past me and never said a word; never gave a flicker of recognition. We don't see each other too often, but we do know each other casually. Did he deliberately snub me? Did he not hear me? Did he forget who I was? Should I be angry? Hurt? Embarrassed? These thoughts and feelings welled up within me, and I had to accurately process the internal and external data and come up with a response that was pleasing to God. On the way to the car I concluded that he must have been concentrating on someone else at the time, and simply did not hear me or see me. That's all there was to it. I won't let it bother me.

That's discernment at work. In some situations discernment takes time. We need to be willing to take the time and invest the effort. In other situations, we accomplish it in a split second. Sometimes it is not until the situation is over that we realize with discernment how we should have handled it. That's growth. At other times we are so used to this kind of event that we automatically react in a way that is proper. For example, when we see the flashing red lights on a school bus, we don't have to stop and discern. We just stop! God's Word recognizes that life situations offer us the challenge of deciding what to do, and that this process of deciding or discerning is an area where we should be growing.

We may be tempted to skip the discernment process. It

takes too much time and effort. We've been this route before; we know what to do; we're traveling down the highway of life on "cruise control." Maybe so, but perhaps there are enough new features for us to pause, ponder, and probe. God expects us to walk wisely. We may not always be able to do that automatically.

On the other hand, there are those who go through life always discerning and never deciding. God expects us to know, discern, and act. In so doing, we will make mistakes; but he who never made a mistake never made a discovery. My goal: to be a person who thinks and acts with discernment. This is one of the many areas of personal growth that takes top priority. [4]

Emotions

Name a feeling that is inherently wrong for a believer to have. Exercise discernment before you answer! Let me suggest that the right response is that there are none. No feeling, of itself, is wrong. Any feeling can be right and any feeling can be wrong, depending on why we experience it and how we express it. The joy of our salvation is right. Rejoicing when your opponent is embarrassed is wrong. Anger over the effects of sin is legitimate (Mark 3:5). Anger over the puncture of an inflated ego is wrong.

No emotion is more important than any other emotion. God gave us the capacity to experience and express a full range of feelings. It is our responsibility to do this biblically. Take feelings of concern, worry, and anxiety. Are they legitimate? They certainly can be. Christ was "troubled" about Judas's act of betrayal (John 13:21). Paul was "intensely concerned" about believers who were being led into sin (2 Corinthians 11:29). Timothy was commended for his "genuine concern" for other believers (Philippians 2:20). Are you perhaps troubled about a rebellious teenager, a wayward roommate, an unloving husband, an unhappy friend? All these feelings can be valid, yes, even virtuous. God gave us the capacity to be concerned about others. He expects us to use it.

He also gave us the capacity to be concerned about ourselves. He intends for us to use it, too. Christ was troubled about what was going to happen on the cross (John 12:27). It was a new, different, ominous, forbidding event, which would involve personal suffering. He responded humanly, emotionally, and legitimately. You have felt the same way when taking a test in school, going for a job interview, giving a speech, going to the doctor. These feelings are normal. Paul used truth to bring conviction to the sin-saturated Corinthians, the kind of conviction that stabbed them emotionally, that made them feel bad. In the final analysis, it was good for them to feel bad (2 Corinthians 7:8-13).

But there is another side to emotions. Christ told His disciples that He was going to leave them (John 13:31-38). This threw them into an emotional tailspin, the kind of reaction your toddler has when you first leave him with the sitter. The Lord told them they need not feel that way (John 14:1). Just like you reassure your crying toddler. Anxiety can be wrong, and in their case it was.

What did He do to help them deal with their improper feelings? He gave them facts relevant to the situation—facts about where He was going and what He was going to do, and about His return (John 14:2-24). Just like you inform your child. These facts, He said, would allow them to experience peace (John 14:25-27). But since they didn't have all the facts, Christ at the same time encourages them to exercise faith (John 14:1). Do we ever really have all the facts pertinent to a situation? The lack of facts stimulates faith. So, when we are not bringing the truth of God and a trust in God to bear on a given situation, the anxiety we experience will be illegitimate. When we do apply truth and trust, whatever feelings we have will be appropriate.

Imagine yourself a first string forward on the basketball team in your senior year in high school. In the third game of the season you break your ankle, ending your prep basketball career. How do you feel? Not too good. A bit depressed. Slightly frustrated. A little sad. Perhaps even angry. How do you handle these feelings? With facts relevant to your situation. Your ankle is broken. That's a basic fact you need to accept. Your feelings can't change that fact. It could have been worse and it will heal and you will run and jump again. These are also pertinent facts. They ought to affect your feelings—positively. Why my ankle? Why this year? You'll not get facts that will satisfactorily answer those questions. You will be told that "God causes all things to work together for good"—that's a fact you'll have to put your faith in, and when you do your feelings will be legitimate and you will have peace.

Consulting with someone you trust is a basic way to get facts and exercise faith. The Bible calls this prayer. It tells us to "be anxious for nothing, but in everything by prayer and supplication with thanksgiving let your requests be made known to God" (Philippians 4:6). The result is a peace which surpasses all comprehension; that is, it includes the facts but goes beyond into the realm of faith (4:7).

A distraught, widowed Christian mother, battling with depression and alcohol finally gave up, shut the garage door, started the car, and asphyxiated herself. The fumes seeped through the furnace duct into the bedroom above and took the life of her lovely, innocent, recently converted Christian teenage daughter. I knew both of them. My emotions ran the gamut. Anger. Sorrow. Everything in between. My mind screamed out for facts, facts that would answer all the questions. The girl and her mother are in heaven. God is sovereign. God is good. He makes no mistakes. Those were the only facts that came. That left a lot of room for faith. I experienced peace in the midst of deep feelings. Peace is not always the absence of emotions.

Christians are to be emotional—emotionally sensitive and emotionally stable. My goal: to be a person of deep, disciplined feelings. This is another area of personal growth that takes top priority.

By the Way . . .

Love yourself! Do it by finding out what God says you need to know and do with reference to yourself.

Find out what *faith* is and how you can put it into practice.

Learn how to *pray* and do it.

Discover what *pride* is and get rid of it.

Develop a *self-concept* that is adequate and accurate.

Clarify your *values.*

Identify your *talents.*

Probe the fact, meaning, and use of your *sexuality.*

Face the fact that you engage in frequent *self-decep-tion.*

Reflect on the truth that you are made in the *image of God.*

Use your *spiritual gift.*

Clear your *conscience.*

Feel deeply.

Enjoy *life.*

Face *death.*

Treat your *body* right.

Conquer the *flesh.*

Depend on the *Holy Spirit.*

Be *humble.*

Sounds like a self-centered curriculum. It is, because that is exactly what we need. God wants to invade and transform every area of our life so that we can impact ourselves, our world, our church, our home, our government, and our job according to His will. If I don't give myself top priority, that will not happen.

Chapter Eight, Notes

[1]J. I. Packer, *Knowing God* (Downers Grove, Ill.: Inter-Varsity Press, 1973), p. 6.

[2]H. Haarbeck, "dokimos," *The New International Dictionary of New Testament Theology,* ed. Colin Brown, III (1978), 808.

[3]Other passages that deal with this concept of discernment are 1 Corinthians 11:28; 2 Corinthians 13:5; Galatians 6:4; Ephesians 5:10; Philippians 1:10; 1 John 4:1.

[4]1 Kings 3 is an instructive portion of Scripture on discernment. Solomon recognized that the essence of leadership was decision making and asked God for "an understanding heart . . . to discern between good and evil" (3:9). That request was pleasing in God's sight (3:10).

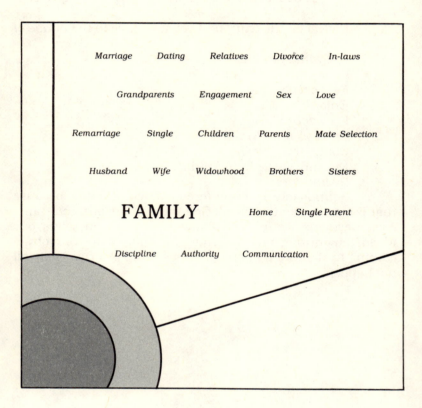

Marriage Dating Relatives Divorce In-laws

Grandparents Engagement Sex Love

Remarriage Single Children Parents Mate Selection

Husband Wife Widowhood Brothers Sisters

FAMILY Home Single Parent

Discipline Authority Communication

CHAPTER NINE

You and Your Family

Expanding Awareness

Physical birth creates a whole new set of significant family relationships. When the first baby is born it becomes a son or a daughter with a new dad and mom, and new sets of grandparents and uncles and aunts and cousins. When spiritual birth takes place, it too makes an impact on the family, for it adds new responsibilities in all of these family relationships. For example, when parents become Christians, they then have the privilege and responsibility of rearing their children biblically. When a couple is saved, they can integrate biblical truth into their marriage.

In this chapter we will expand our awareness of these relationships and responsibilities. We have enlarged the family segment of our model at the left.

Perspective

First, let's reiterate our conviction. The family is not more important or less important than other relationships. It is *just as important* as the church, the job, and your other relationships. You're right, we have placed it first in our discussion of significant neighbors, but we didn't do this to indicate that it is more important than the others. We could have placed any of the others first. No hierarchy is intended in our chapter arrangement.

Second, some will no doubt plead for the priority of the

family because it started way back in Genesis, long before the church and human government. Doesn't that make the family more important? No, chronology does not necessarily imply superiority. The world and work came before the family in Genesis. That doesn't make them more important. Heaven comes last on God's timetable. That doesn't make it less important.

Third, you will notice that the words in the family segment on the diagram above identify people, concepts, and functions. A husband is a person who is to take the concept of love and put it into practice with his wife. Communication is a concept we must understand, an activity we must engage in. We must do it with members of our family. The family is more than people. It is people in significant relationships with other people. People who have specific responsibilities in these various relationships.

Fourth, there is no priority system among these family relationships and responsibilities. Parents aren't more important than children. Husbands aren't more important than wives. Marriage isn't more important than singleness. Leaving isn't more important than cleaving. Loving isn't more important than training. Submission isn't more important than headship. There are biblical instructions in each of these areas. That makes each of them important and imperative.

Fifth, the items identified in the above family segment are selective. Each one could be broken down into numerous particulars. For example, relatives: aunts, uncles, cousins, nephews, nieces, and so on. Other issues and items could be listed, such as adoption, birth control, handicapped persons, premarital counseling, homosexuality, unity, sex education, alimony. A lot of things are tied to the family. What we need to do is determine our current family relationships and responsibilities and discharge them.

You As a Person
As a child you are responsible to honor and obey your parents (Ephesians 6:1-4). If you have brothers and sisters, you should not operate on an "I'll get even with you" policy (Romans 12:17-18). As a single young person, all of your relationships with the opposite sex should be pure (1 Thessalonians

4:1-8). As you look for a potential mate, you should find another Christian with whom you can develop a biblical marriage (1 Corinthians 7:39). As a single person, you must come to grips adequately with your self-concept, your sexuality, and your spiritual potential (1 Corinthians 7:1-40).

Where are you as a single? Do you know what it means to walk wisely in your relationships with the opposite sex? Are you doing so? Are you, with spiritual discernment, developing a healthy self-concept as a single? Are you handling your sexual drives in harmony with God's commandments? If you have been widowed or divorced, are you—with biblical discernment—thinking the right thoughts, experiencing the right feelings, doing the right activities?

While you are single, regardless of how old you are and regardless of how long your single state lasts, you have a number of biblical responsibilities. It is your obligation to know them and do them. For you, they are top priority. Don't get lulled into thinking that you can only really do God's will when and if you marry.

You As a Partner

Marriage is a partnership. Partnerships are successful when both persons do what they are supposed to do. Not just now and then, or at the point of crisis, but regularly. Husbands are to love and lead (Ephesians 5:25-33). Wives are to submit and respect (Ephesians 5:22-24, 33). Both partners are to leave, cleave, and develop unity (Genesis 2:24). Both are to give themselves unreservedly to each other sexually (1 Corinthians 7:2-7). Husbands are to seek to understand their wives and to treat them as equals (1 Peter 3:7). When one partner is not a Christian, the other should seek to attract the partner to the Lord with a winsomely appropriate lifestyle (1 Peter 3:1-6). The words that they speak to each other should always be truthful and appropriate, designed to build up rather than tear down, to draw together rather than drive apart (Ephesians 4:25-32).

Partners are still sons and daughters, and have to relate properly to their own parents and to their partner's parents (in-laws). Partners are not perfect and tend to be self-centered, hard to get along with, stubborn, poor communicators, neurotically dependent or ferociously independent, and even unfaithful. These symptoms can appear in any marriage. Partners must be willing to take the steps necessary to prevent or cope with them. If separation or divorce or death occurs, they must deal with a whole array of new feelings and new relationships. If they remarry, they must give significant attention to insure that this new relationship is successful.

Where are you now in your marriage? What biblical responsibilities do you currently have? What areas have you been neglecting? What needs does your partner have that you can meet? Or to borrow from the last chapter, are you developing the capacity to *discern* what needs to be done in your marriage? Are you using your *emotions* productively or are you letting your feelings ruin you and the relationship? Your relationship to your marriage partner is a top priority responsibility. Are you giving it that rating?

You As a Parent

Along came the children and now you have teaching, training, correcting, and controlling responsibilities. (Deuteronomy 6:4-9, Ephesians 6:4). Every time you produce a child, you add another top priority responsibility. Think about that! Children have ongoing, everchanging needs that parents have to meet. Parents have to add these needs to all the other needs they are meeting. You cannot put needs on hold any more than you can put God's commandments on hold. (Well, you can, but you pay the consequences.)

Children need to be played with, read to, walked with, listened to, held close, and as they grow, let go. Parents have to inculcate convictions, not just impose them. Parents have to accept each child with his or her uniqueness. Our temptation is to expect them to be like a brother or sister . . . or like us. Children grieve their parents. Thus, parents worry a lot—often legitimately. Children grow up and leave home and marry. Parents then become in-laws and grandparents and counselors, and sometimes nitpicking, interfering busybodies!

Parenting is a God-given responsibility that takes top priority. Do you know what God expects of you as a parent? Are you putting it into practice? Do you practice parenting only on weekends and vacations or do you see it as an every day, every year responsibility?

Expanding Your Love Ability

We have briefly hovered over the general area of the family and surveyed its components. Now let's land and get out and examine one specific area: love. In an earlier chapter we established the fact that love has a propositional force to it—keeping the commandments; and a personal force—taking the initiative and acting properly (sometimes even sacrificially) to meet legitimate needs.

The truth needs to strike home.

Loving Your Partner

Husbands—love your wives! How do you do that? Take the initiative and act sacrificially to meet her needs.

> What does she need? A man who provides food, clothing, and shelter for her and the kids. Do it.

> She is at home all day carrying on high level conversations with toddlers, with added intellectual stimulus from Sesame Street. Needed? Adult companionship and adult conversation. Provide it. (I know, you've been interacting with adults all day. You need peace and quiet. Sacrifice!)

> She needs to hear words of tender affection, personal approval, affirmation, compliments, even a bit of mushy sentiment. Don't make her go without it. Don't make her beg for it. Take the initiative. Do it. (I know, you'd rather wait for soft lights, dreamy music, and cologne. Sacrifice!)

> She needs the leaky faucet fixed and the curtain rods put up. You've been promising for weeks. Do it. (I know. It's Monday night. Vikings against the Rams. Sacrifice!)

Wives—love your husbands! You do it the same way. Take the initiative and act sacrificially to meet his needs.

He needs his lunch packed. Do it. He needs
variety in the menu; something besides carrot
sticks and peanut butter sandwiches. Take
the initiative. Surprise him. He needs more
than food. Write him a love note on the napkin.
Or on the banana. (I know. You'd have to get
up ten minutes earlier to get creative with the
menu, and you're not adept at writing love
notes on napkins, much less on bananas.
Sacrifice!)

He needs to talk about his work. His fears and
frustrations. His achievements and his
dreams. Open his verbal valve. Ask him
questions. Give him your undivided attention.
(I know. Your big guy is Mr. Macho. The
strong, silent type. But he needs to talk. Pry
him open. You can do it. Even if it involves
. . . sacrifice!)

Function like this in your marriage and it will cut
down on nagging, because nagging is the reaction of a person
whose needs are not being met. Engage in need-meeting activities like these and you weave solid strands into your relationship, the kind of strands that can handle the things that
seek to wedge in between and drive you apart. Every time you
act to meet his or her needs you are saying in a powerful, profound way, "Sweetheart, I love you." And remember this: When
it is harder to take the initiative, and it involves more sacrifice
on your part, you are probably meeting deeper needs in your
partner's life. If it is easy for you to love your mate, you may not
be doing a very good job!

Loving Your Child
Parents—love your children!
What do teenagers need? They are convinced they need
few, if any, rules. Lots of time at the wheel of the family car (or
better yet, their own auto). Unrestricted time on the telephone.
The right to put others down (especially teachers, parents, and
younger brothers and sisters). Freedom to mumble a totally
unsatisfactory answer when asked, "Where did you go?" (Out)

"What did you do?" (Nothing).

As parents, you must discern which needs are legitimate and what actions are proper to meet those needs. Or to put it another way, you must determine what commandments of God you are going to obey with reference to your teen, and what commandments of God they must obey.

For example, the Word of God says that "all bitterness and wrath and anger and clamor and slander be put away from you, along with all malice" (Ephesians 4:31). That puts some basic restrictions on teenagers who bad-mouth others. It also puts a responsibility on parents who have teens who engage in verbal assault (Ephesians 6:4). They need to obey the Word. If they are not obeying, they need to be confronted. If they are, they need to be commended. The apostle Paul engaged in both confronting and commending (cf. 1 Corinthians 1:10-17, 2 Thessalonians 1:3-4). The young person who is putting others down needs to be gently but firmly reminded that such behavior is wrong. That's one way you love a teenager! If you have an emerging adult, his or her behavior is a top priority responsibility—for both of you. They may not realize this. The parents must. That will inevitably involve . . . sacrifice.

Your kids are younger. Toddlers maybe. What do they need? Go ahead, say it. They need to grow up! We seek to accelerate this process with words like, "Sit up like a lady," or "Act like a man." There's nothing wrong with encouraging growth, but to expect a little boy to become a man immediately upon our request is a bit unrealistic. So, along with the need to grow up, the child needs to be *accepted* right where he or she is.

This involves sacrifice, because it isn't easy for an adult to step back down into the child's world. But that's the way you love preschoolers. You take the initiative and act sacrificially to meet their needs. They need to be held. To be listened to. To be played with. To be read to. They need their shoes tied, their hair braided, their toys fixed, their bike repaired, their questions answered, their school papers read.

One evening after supper, I settled into my easy chair with a good book and began to immerse myself in its stimulating, stretching, theological insights. Down the hall and into the room came our three-year-old blond bombshell, Juli. "Daddy," she said, "will you read to me?" I looked at the book I was reading—*The Providence of God* by G. C. Berkouwer, translated from the Dutch. I looked at the book she was holding in her pudgy little hand—*Myrtle the Turtle!*

That's when love stops being sentiment and theory. Are you going to shoo the kid off with some lame excuse, or put your book down and let her crawl into your lap while you crawl into her world of turtles? That's a sacrifice for an adult who has long since graduated from children's literature. That night I sacrificed Berkouwer for Myrtle and we labored through the eighteen pages of a not very thick plot. I could see the end coming. I started reaching for my book, waiting for Juli to slip down off my lap and run and play. No way. Instead, she looked up at me with those big blue eyes and said, "Daddy, read it again." That's because a child needs repetition. I don't. Once through *Myrtle the Turtle* meets my needs for months. But parental love must be willing to sacrifice some of its own needs in order to meet the needs of the child.

This does not mean that we allow our children to dominate us to the extent that we fail to meet our own basic needs. A mother who picks up her child every time he cries will eventually fail to meet her own legitimate needs for privacy, relaxation, and time with her husband. The child may think he needs to be held at any time of the day or night, but that is not a legitimate need. The parent who does it is not acting properly to meet his needs or the child's.

Loving Your Parents

Children—love your parents!

What do your parents need? Nothing. They are grown up. Grown-ups have everything they need. Right? Oh, no, they don't! They need letters like this.

> MOTHER:
>   I was just sitting here thinking and the thought just struck me: how in the world did you cook for SIX (6) people for so many years???? I mean, I just realized what a *drag* that must have been. I don't see how you could stand it.
>   This must mean I'm maturing—realizing

and appreciating these kinds of things that
you did all those years without complaining. I
guess that was because you loved us, huh?
   Oh well. I LOVE YOU
MOMMMMMMMYYYYYY!!!!!!!!
XOXOXOXOX
Beth

That's from our twenty-one-year-old daughter, out of
college and living and working on her own in Seattle. That letter met a mother's deeper needs. Audrey read it over and over.
Then she read it to everybody who would listen. Then she
framed it. It wasn't easy for Beth to write it. It involved a certain
amount of . . . sacrifice.

Explore the ramifications of this kind of agape love.
What needs do in-laws have? The need to be invited over
periodically? The need to be consulted for their mature advice
on occasion? The need to be graciously told that their offer to
help is much appreciated, but you will arrange the living room
on your own? Words like that are not easy, right? Not easy for
you to speak; not easy for them to receive. But love doesn't do
what's easy. Love does what's necessary and right. "Learn to
engage in good deeds to meet pressing needs" (Titus 3:14).
That's good Pauline poetry.

By the Way . . .

The point is frequently made that the home takes
priority over the church because in 1 Timothy (3:4, 5, 12) it is
clearly taught that a man's performance in the home qualifies
or disqualifies him for leadership in the church. But the passage doesn't say anything about the family being more important than the church. It is simply emphasizing that the home
is a major proving ground wherein we can evaluate the quality
of a man's skill and faithfulness as a husband and father.

The church is just as important as the family because
it is a major context for equipping men with the Word of God so
they can function rightly in the home, demonstrate leadership
quality, and become church leaders (2 Timothy 3:16-17, Titus
1:9). Furthermore, the world is just as important a proving
ground as the home, for the acceptable church leader "must

have a good reputation with those outside the church" (1 Timothy 3:7). Once again, we see the weakness of trying to sequentialize biblical responsibilities.

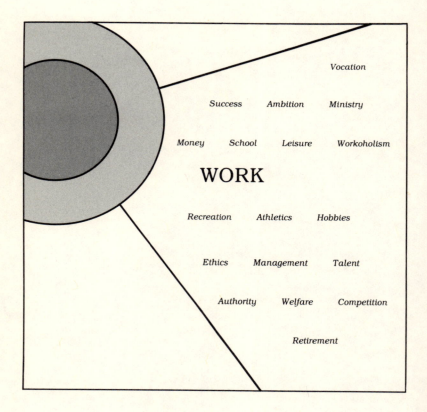

CHAPTER TEN

You and Your Work

Expanding Awareness

You spend a lot of time on the job. You expend a lot of physical, mental, and emotional energy on the job. And, realize it or not, you traffic in a lot of truth on the job. That's what this chapter is all about—the time, the energy, and the truth that are related to the job. But first, let's broaden the boundaries. We have listed some of the things that can be associated with the general area of work at the left.

Perspective

We need to make some observations. First, work is another one of the important areas of life. It doesn't come *below* or *above* any of the other categories; it is *along with* the other biblically significant segments. God expects me to act in certain ways with my family and He expects me to act in certain ways on my job. Because they are both divine expectations, they are both human obligations. Each has top priority.

Second, my vocation—what I do for a living—is one significant item in the work segment. It is important that I accurately assess my God-given talents and find a job where I can develop and use these capacities. There are some jobs that would be wrong for me as a Christian to engage in. For example, work requiring dishonesty, endeavors that take unfair advantage of people, and businesses that violate civil law. These are not low priority jobs—they are "off the approved list" jobs. There are many jobs "on the approved list." Though these jobs are different in nature and make different contributions to society, they are all important because each and every one can be done to the glory of God. A millwright and a mailman don't do the same thing, but they each do important and significant things.

Third, you'll notice a lot of other items besides vocation listed in the work segment. That's because work involves and relates to many different things. School prepares us for work. Disability (or laziness) keeps us from work. Retirement ends our formal work. Recreation and hobbies are forms of work we engage in without pay. Money is something we earn at work. Ambition and competition motivate our work. Many of our work decisions have ethical implications. Leisure and rest provide a welcome break from work. The general area of work is a multifaceted area of relationships and responsibilities. When a facet touches us, it becomes a top priority.

Fourth, this list is selective. You could add many other areas such as labor unions, unemployment, pensions, career changes, vocational guidance, automation, capitalism, profit, working wives, fringe benefits, moonlighting, investing, vacations, strikes, quotas, technology, incentives. You could take any one area and explore it more thoroughly. Consider school, for example. This area would involve such things as formulating biblical perspectives on teachers, students, tests, grades, popularity, liberal arts vs. specialization, whether to go to college or not, or extracurricular activities like athletics and all the pressures that go along with making the team, playing the game, and winning and losing. How about a sermon on "A Theology of Benchwarming" or "How To Handle a Losing Season"? (Or winning season, as the case may be.) Or how about a Bible study on materialism, or bankruptcy, or free enterprise, or on jobs that involve travel?

Fifth, the work segment above is not designed to represent *time.* If it were, it would be a lot larger than the other segments in our diagram. This is simply another relationship/responsibility segment, a segment in which we do invest large quantities of time. That doesn't make our work more important than other neighbor relationships. *Time is not synonymous with importance.* You can spend eight hours behind a desk giving quality attention to your job and five minutes on the phone giving quality attention to your mate. Both are important!

Sixth, overlap is inherent in this model. You work to provide the necessities of life for *yourself* and your *family.* A certain percentage of your income can be channeled into the *church.* Skills developed on the job can be utilized in the ministry of the church. The *satanic world system* has filtered into every aspect of your job and is seeking to get you to compromise. *Government* regulations impinge in some way on nearly every transaction that takes place in your business. Overlap can have positive implications. It can also have insidiously detrimental results. The working man who spends long hours on the job, doing it well and making money, may be neglecting his responsibilities as a husband and father. The insidious part of it is that he may convince himself he is doing it all for his wife and family. He is showing his love by seldom showing up.

A Biblical Concept of Work

It all started in Genesis. Men and women were created and blessed by God with the capacity, responsibility, and need to work. Three words delineate the job description of the first couple and for all their progeny. The first is in Genesis 1:28, "Be fruitful and multiply, and fill the earth, and *subdue* it." *Subdue* means to bring under control. It assumes the one being subdued is hostile and thus there is the need for correction.[1] The other two words are found in Genesis 2:15, "Then the LORD God took the man and put him into the garden of Eden to cultivate it and keep it." *Cultivate* refers to the work in the garden which facilitated the growth of crops. *Keep* emphasizes the work of preserving, guarding, and caring for. Elsewhere it is used to describe the activity of "tending the sheep."[2]

Before the fall, was every day a holiday? A continual vacation without vocation? Not on your life! God built into the world the need for control. Nature is not passive, it is active. It must be brought under subjection and kept under subjection. The very fact of seasons mean that there are periods of dormancy and periods of growth. During dormancy we plow and plant. During growth we till, water, prune, trim, and harvest. Built into God's original creation is a *challenge*. Creation does not do man's will gladly, easily, or automatically.

Even in the garden of Eden bushes had to be trimmed, plants had to be thinned, berries had to be picked, leaves had to be raked, and friendly animals had to be kept from tromping all over the petunias! The original world was not a work-free environment, nor was the work just busy work to occupy time. It was part of God's plan, built into His world, assigned to His creatures, and classified as a blessing.

That was before sin entered the scene. The curse outlined in Genesis 3:17-19 cannot be the introduction of work or even the introduction of hard work. Sin and the resultant curse brought disorder into the world, making work difficult, demanding, frustrating, and unending. The curse added negative dimensions to a positive concept.

The world was created to be worked on: to be controlled, preserved, explored, developed, and used. The domination given to man is not just physical but mental. God put the minerals in the ground. We have to use our minds and bodies to get them out and convert them into usable products. This is a "do-it-yourself" world. Work is inherent in it. Seeds have to be planted. Oil has to be pumped and refined. Trees have to be logged. Water has to be stored and channeled. Music has to be written and played. Theories have to be developed and tested.

Dishes get dirty and have to be washed. Clothes get soiled and have to be cleaned. Kids get hungry and have to be fed. Debris settles and has to be swept. This all adds up . . . to housework. Holes have to be drilled, screws have to be tightened, boxes have to be filled, things have to be moved, counted, stacked, opened, closed, recorded. People have to be hired, trained, paid, evaluated, waited on. It all adds up to work. Students have to subdue textbooks—and sometimes their own lazy, wandering minds. We have to subdue leaky faucets, broken appliances, unwelcome bugs, fast growing weeds. Work is ubiquitous.

Is your work exciting and fulfilling? God made it that way. Is your work hard? God put that challenge into it. Is your work frustrating, boring, repetitive, even frightening? It could be the result of the curse. It could be your attitude. Maybe you need to change your job. Maybe you need to change your attitude. Maybe you need to do both! Work is integral to our well-being and to God's program. That perspective deserves top priority.

A Biblical Concept of Vocation

Let me take a few moments to plant some thoughts about vocation in your mind.[3] You can water and fertilize them (or dig them up). What do you enjoy doing? What do you do well? Your answers to these questions identify what I would call your talents. That's assuming you are old enough to know what you enjoy doing and have had enough experience to determine what you do with skill. I'm not talking about spiritual gifts. They are given at salvation and equip the believer to function uniquely in the body of Christ. I am talking about natural talents. I think they are there at our physical birth, and as we grow we can discover, develop, and use them in any area—and potentially in every area—of our lives.

Where do these talents come from? Well, we inherit our characteristics from our parents, but sovereignly superintending this process is the Creator. Two passages of Scripture are instructive here. The first is in Psalm 139 where the creative work of God is linked to the embryonic beginnings of the human person.

> For Thou didst form my inward parts;
> Thou didst weave me in my mother's womb.
> I will give thanks to Thee, for I am fearfully
>   and wonderfully made;
> Wonderful are Thy works,
> And my soul knows it very well.
> My frame was not hidden from Thee,
> When I was made in secret,
> And skillfully wrought in the depths of the
>   earth.
> Thine eyes have seen my unformed
>   substance;
> And in Thy book they were all written,
> The days that were ordained for me,

When as yet there was not one of them
(Psalm 139:13-16).

.This text tells us that God is the ultimate author of
your physical being. Whether you are short or tall, slim or
stocky, fast or slow can be traced to the workmanship of God.
The ability to hear with perfect pitch, to speak with resonant
tones, to draw with pen in hand, to throw with accuracy, or to
kick the ball a country mile is all part of the creative handiwork
of God. No wonder the psalmist concluded that he was fear-
fully, wonderfully, and skillfully made.

Today we use different terms. We say so and so is
talented, has a knack for it, is proficient, has experience. Follow it back to its source—God. And be sure to look at the vocational implications. We ought to do our best to be in vocations
that utilize our talents.

The second passage of Scripture is found in Isaiah
64:8.

But now, O LORD, Thou art our Father,
We are the clay, and Thou our potter;
And all of us are the work of Thy hand.

Isaiah said the same thing David said, but in a different way.
God, the Master Potter, has fashioned each of us to be exactly
the way He wanted us to be. The clay and the potter's wheel will
produce nothing without the designing touch of the potter's
hands. Those sovereign hands have sculpted you into a
unique person, a person endowed with a rich variety of God-
ordained capacities—natural talents.

Are you an organizer, a creative dreamer, an aggressive innovator, a problem solver, one who likes to build or re-
pair things, an artist, a musician, a writer, one who enjoys
working with numbers, a skilled athlete, one who is adept at
promoting, selling, analyzing, synthesizing? These are God-
given talents. Nobody has all of them. Everybody has some of
them. It is our responsibility to discover our talents, to accept
them as from God, to develop them through education and
training, and to use them for His glory. That, in a nutshell, is
what a good, biblically-centered vocational guidance program
should do. Wherever possible, we should attempt to work in

areas that tap our talents. Even periods of leisure and recreation ought to be opportunities to express and enjoy our talents. And when we tend to be disappointed and even dissatisfied because we are not omni-talented or do not have a certain talent, it would be well to remember the words of Isaiah: "Woe to the one who quarrels with his Maker" (Isaiah 45:9). The clay doesn't talk back. Vocational choices ought to be viewed as top priority decisions.

Ethics on the Job

How you do your work is just as important as what work you do. Work involves competition and rewards. One reward is money. Another is status. When we are competing for money and status, there will be a subtle and powerful temptation to be . . . *unethical.*

Phil is a Christian young man who has recently gone to work for a small but growing electronics plant. He is in sales and will be dealing mainly with aircraft and computer companies manufacturing the same products. Phil is an aggressive, confident, ambitious person who wants to be successful in his job and at the same time wants to honor the Lord with his attitudes and actions. What pressures will Phil have to be unethical?

He'll have pressures associated with selling, traveling, expense accounts, entertaining, price cutting, kickbacks, quotas, delivery dates, product comparison, profanity, alcohol, materialism, commissions, long hours, promotions, honesty, witness, lifestyle, women, deadlines, and on and on. Phil is working in an environment saturated with ethical decisions. It is his responsibility to know what is right and to do what is right. This responsibility can't be assigned some number on a priority list and attended to after he has served his term on the church finance committee and raised his children. Eight hours a day, five days a week, it takes top priority.

Every job has its ethical implications. That's why Peter exhorts servants, in their relationship to their masters, to "do what is right." Every Christian employer and employee has to daily determine what is right and do it. That will involve suffering (1 Peter 2:18-20).

By the Way . . .

What is "the Lord's work"? We hear announcements on Sunday asking lay people in the congregation to get involved in "the Lord's work." That is, to teach a Sunday school class, to serve on a committee, to be an usher, to give more generously, or to furnish 4,000 cookies for VBS. "The Lord's work" here is obviously serving in the church. On other occasions we hear and read persuasive invitations to "go into the Lord's work"—meaning, of course, to commit ourselves to fulltime vocational Christian service.

So far so good. The Lord's work is definitely serving in the church and serving in the professional ministry. But don't stop there. The Lord's work is anything you do that can bring glory to Him. You're doing the Lord's work any time you obey the commandments; any time you are acting properly to meet legitimate needs. So you can do the Lord's work at home, in the church, in the world, as a citizen, on the job, and even while meditating alone.

Chapter Ten, Notes

[1]Similar uses of "subdue" can be seen in Joshua 18:1; Jeremiah 34:11; Numbers 32:22, 29; and Esther 7:8. I am indebted to my colleague, Dr. Robert Hughes, for his many probing insights into the biblical doctrine of work.

[2]Cf. 1 Samuel 25:16; Genesis 3:24, 4:9, 30:31, 2 Samuel 15:16.

[3]For fresh, helpful information on vocational guidance, see John D. Bradley, *Christian Career Planning* (Portland, Ore.: Multnomah Press, 1977). Career guidance tools, designed to help individuals discover and use their God-given talents and accept their God-given limitations, are being eveloped by IDAK Research Associates, Inc., 7931 N.E. Halsey, Portland, OR 97213. Write them for further information.

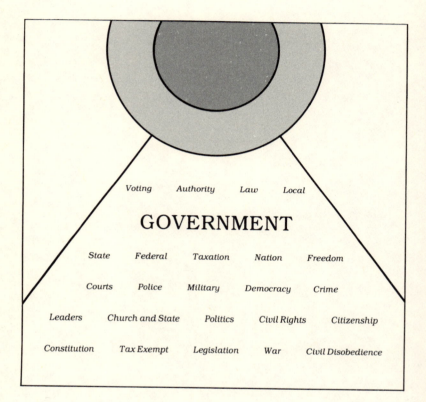

Voting   Authority   Law   Local

GOVERNMENT

State   Federal   Taxation   Nation   Freedom

Courts   Police   Military   Democracy   Crime

Leaders   Church and State   Politics   Civil Rights   Citizenship

Constitution   Tax Exempt   Legislation   War   Civil Disobedience

You and Government

Expanding Awareness

The church and the state. The believer and politics. Sanctification and legislation. Eternal security and maximum security. Renew your mind and renew your license. Bible conferences and summit conferences. The right to worship and the right to work. The will of God and zoning restrictions. In the past, Christians have been vitally interested in the former and nominally concerned about the latter, the latter areas being either too worldly for or not worthy of their attention. But things are changing, and I desire this chapter to facilitate the change. At the left are some of the issues which fall within the area of government.

Perspective

First, *nations* are a distinct part of God's program. From the original human being, Adam, God made "every nation of mankind to live on all the face of the earth, having determined their appointed times, and the boundaries of their habitation" (Acts 17:26). The confusion of language at the tower of Babel was one of the ways God facilitated the formation of separate national entities (Genesis 11:1-9). Behind the creation, preservation, modification, and even the eradication of nations looms the sovereign hand of God.

Second, *human government* is a God-ordained institution. The authority to govern as well as the particular governing authority is established by God (Romans 13:1). The responsibility of human beings to investigate, prosecute, and execute is embryonically outlined in Genesis 9:5-6 and then developed more thoroughly in the Mosaic Law (Exodus 20-22). Christians cannot lightly regard government, its fact and its function.

Third, every believer is to be a *responsible citizen.* That's because every believer is a citizen and every believer has God-given citizenship responsibilities. There are no exceptions to citizenship and there are no levels of citizenship. *Every person* is to be in subjection to the governing authorities (Romans 13:1). Biblical citizenship is a top priority responsibility for every Christian.

Fourth, the believer's relationship to government is *just as important* as his relationship to other areas. Let me illustrate from Scripture. In 1 Peter 2:13, Christian citizens are told to submit to human government. In 1 Peter 2:18, Christian slaves are told to submit to their masters. In 1 Peter 3:1, Christian wives are told to submit to their husbands. Now, suppose one of the readers of Peter's letter was a Christian female slave married to an unbeliever. And suppose you were there at the time, and she came to you and said, "I am a new Christian and I want to make sure my priorities are straight. Which one of these three areas of submission should I put first?"

What would your answer be? Would you tell her first to concentrate on submitting to her husband until she wins him to the Lord? And then she should turn her attention to doing what she is told at work, and when she feels she has done that long enough to earn a raise and a promotion, she ought to stop driving her chariot so fast and use whip signals when she turns?

I hope not. I hope you'd simply say, "Peter doesn't assign any priority. Each of the three commands to submit carries the full weight of God's authority. Work on each one of them. Every day."

The believer's responsibility to government is neither more nor less important than any other area. It is just as important.

Fifth, the very *nature* of government causes it to touch

the other main areas of Christian responsibility. It provides religious freedom for the individual and the church. It limits the power of business and industry. It protects the rights of the family. It seeks to control the immorality in a fallen world. In many ways it fulfills its biblical mandate to reward the good and punish the bad (Romans 13:1-7).

But there is a deepening concern among many today that instead of controlling the satanic world system, government is slowly but surely being permeated by that system. Overlapping which was positive and protective has instead become a negative, harmful undercutting. For example, the Supreme Court of the State of Washington has ruled in favor of a fifteen year old who asked to be taken from her parents because of differences of opinion concerning her dating, her friends, and her desire to smoke.[1] This kind of judicial overlapping can blur the distinction between the authority of the state and the authority of the parents. Silent, isolated Christians will do little to challenge this encroachment.

Sixth, the issues and areas listed in the goverment segment are just the tip of a huge iceberg. Each one could be amplified and explored. Many others could be added: gun control, abortion, censorship, welfare, lobbying, child abuse, ACLU, sexual discrimination, pornography, statism, bureaucracy, impeachment, appointment vs. election, perjury, dictatorship, the oath, prohibition, jurisprudence vs. legisprudence, civil service, IRS, civil defense, nuclear war, conscientious objection, right to privacy, protest, pacifism—the list is endless.

Seventh, every issue and area within the government segment of our diagram is important. All legislation is important. Every court decision is important. All these issues and areas may not be equally important to you. But because they are activities of divinely-ordained government which affect the lives of people made in the image of God—they are important. It is our task to determine if and how an issue relates to us and others about whom we are concerned. And it is our task to decide what we need to do about it.

Suppose there is a bond issue coming up in the next election. If it passes, your schools will keep providing quality education and excellent extracurricular activities for your kids—but your taxes will go up. If it is defeated, teachers will be laid off, classes will be larger, and athletic and music programs will be pared down. But your taxes won't increase. I can't tell you how to vote, but I can say that you do need to be informed and you do need to vote. Remember our definition of love? Action to meet needs. We can love ourselves, our children, and our neighbors by casting an intelligent ballot.

In the same election you will be choosing a new mayor. The candidate who is well-known and expected to win has clearly indicated that his value system is different from yours, and at certain points, obviously unbiblical. From your standpoint, the other candidate would be a better choice. Okay, now it's up to you to function as a responsible, biblically-oriented citizen. "Yeah," you say, "I'm sure not voting for so-and-so next month." Is that it? That's the extent of your involvement? How about writing some letters? Making some phone calls? Stuffing some envelopes? Delivering some hand-bills?

What's that you say? Oh, I see. You're too involved at church right now . . . taking a course . . . on biblical citizenship.

Scriptural Data

Romans 13:1-7 is a basic text dealing with civil government, but it is by no means the only text. When you look at the Old and New Testaments through a "government grid," you will discover many explicit and implicit references to the subject. Culver expresses this cogently:

> . . . civil government appears on several levels
> in the Scriptures. On the basic level it is *a*
> *fact of biblical history* . . . a topic of preaching
> and writing by the prophets of Judah and
> Israel . . . the subject of divine legislation in
> several important sections of the Pentateuch,
> and a matter for *reflection* by the authors of
> the books of biblical wisdom. On still another
> level, it is a matter of *special instruction,*
> wherein not only our Lord but the prophets
> and apostles provide the essential ingredients

of a doctrine of civil government. Finally, there are the *New Testament exhortations and warnings* to Christians with regard to their response to and duties toward governments, their laws, agencies, and representatives.[2]

Other biblical doctrines must also be brought to bear on the issue of government. For example, the doctrine of sin will cause us to recognize not only the need for human government but the inability of government to ever perfect society. Government carries out its functions in the world—a world composed of both people and things, good and bad. Thus the complex doctrine of the world must be linked to government. The doctrine of Satan must be reckoned with, too, for his claim to be in charge of all the kingdoms of the world was no idle claim (Matthew 4:8-9). There is an immense amount of biblical truth that is relevant to government. This truth is a significant part of the Scripture that is inspired by God and profitable for every believer to know and do. It, too, is top priority truth.

Expanding Involvement

"Law and politics are uncomfortable and largely unfamiliar terrain for the church and for people of piety."[3] Why? Why the discomfort with politics? Why the lack of familiarity with legal issues? It's because we have adopted the "separational model" says Webber, a model that sees the church as radically different from the world and thus to be radically separated from the world.[4] The results—Christians who are at best aloof from government and politics; and at worst, afraid of them.

Consequently our concept of truth is truncated. We focus on the "truth of creation, the truth of the virgin birth, the truth of Christ's miracles, Christ's substitutionary death, and His coming again."[5] We haven't consistently and effectively focused God's truth on political and governmental issues. We isolate. Sin escalates.

Whitehead's words are apropos:

Noninvolvement . . . is choosing to allow
humanism to proceed unrestrained.
Noninvolvement is, therefore, negative

> involvement. If the church continues its
> silence, the only option will be to capitulate
> and be dominated by a humanistic culture
> that will not tolerate Christianity.[6]

"Will not tolerate Christianity." Weigh the impact of those words. We are in a struggle for survival. Our freedoms, even our lives may be at stake. We must activate our belief system and penetrate the world with it. We must come out of hiding and expose and explain our commitment to truth. This means we write letters to the editor. As believers we become informed on candidates' positions, voting records, and other qualifications for office. We campaign for candidates we believe in. We attend and speak out in political science classes, at PTA meetings, at political rallies, at civic clubs, at labor union meetings, at trade association conventions. We use radio, television, and the printed page to present a viable point of view. We encourage civil servants who are doing a good job. When we think they are not, we let them know. We do all of these things—boldly and wisely—because we are Christian citizens with a biblical responsibility to be involved.

By the Way . . .

This is a hard chapter for me to write. I am as uninvolved in biblical citizenship as other Christians. Involvement means front-line duty. Front-line duty means you get shot at. When it comes to getting shot at, I am your basic, Christian coward. I don't like to fight. I don't like to get hit. I don't like to get hurt. I know that as long as I am uninformed and uninvolved, I am safe. I don't have to suffer.

Then I read 1 Peter. It tells me that a Spirit-filled, Word-oriented saint will be on the front lines, doing what is right, and suffering.[7] It is hard for me to read and think and discuss in the realm of politics. There are other things I would rather do. It is hard for me to take a firm, intelligent stand on a political issue. It is even harder for me to make it public, and defend it, and have it criticized and ridiculed. In the area of government my comfort zone is way behind the front lines.

How about yours? Maybe what we both need to do is volunteer for some front-line duty while we are still allowed to carry weapons.

Chapter Eleven, Notes

[1]John W. Whitehead, *The Second American Revolution* (Eligin, Ill.: David C. Cook Publishing Co., 1982), p. 64.

[2]Robert Duncan Culver, *Toward a Biblical View of Civil Government* (Chicago: Moody Press, 1974), pp. 61-62.

[3]Lynn R. Buzzard, *Freedom and Faith* (Westchester, Ill.: Crossway Books, 1982), p. 7.

[4]Robert E. Webber, *The Secular Saint* (Grand Rapids: Zondervan Publishing House, 1979), pp. 75-77.

[5]Francis A. Schaeffer, *A Christian Manifesto* (Westchester, Ill.: Crossway Books, 1981), pp. 19-20.

[6]Whitehead, *The Second American Revolution*, p. 42.

[7]Peter reminds his readers of their status—resident aliens (1:1, 2:11); their lifestyle—holiness (1:13-16); their responsibility—to do what is right (2:15, 20; 3:6, 13, 17; 4:19); and the results—glory to God (2:12, 4:16) and personal suffering (2:20, 3:14-17, 4:19, 5:9-10).

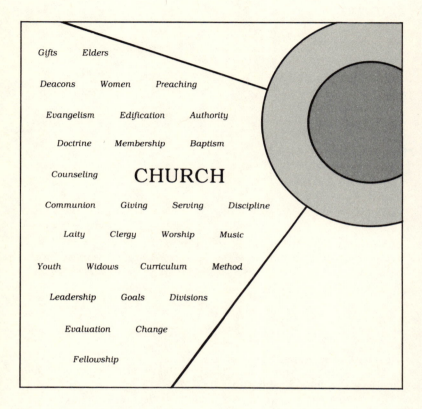

Gifts   Elders

Deacons   Women   Preaching

Evangelism   Edification   Authority

Doctrine   Membership   Baptism

Counseling   CHURCH

Communion   Giving   Serving   Discipline

Laity   Clergy   Worship   Music

Youth   Widows   Curriculum   Method

Leadership   Goals   Divisions

Evaluation   Change

Fellowship

You and the Church

Expanding Awareness

The church—it's something we go to, something we meet in, something we support, and . . . something we are. It is another strategic area of relationships and responsibilities. Like all the others, this slice of our priority pie has a multitude of ingredients in it. At the left are some of them.

Perspective

First, the church is another top priority responsibility for every believer. The Bible doesn't pit the church against anything but sin. It isn't the church *or* the family. It isn't the church *then* the job. The New Testament doesn't say to love your brother or sister in the body, then love your mate, then love your children, then love your unsaved neighbor. The New Testament says to do each and every one of them.

Which is more important: to pray for those in authority over you in the government (1 Timothy 2:1-2), or to pray for those in the church (Ephesians 6:18), or to pray for your own anxieties (Philippians 4:6)? Which is more important: for the church to honor widows (1 Timothy 5:3), or for children to honor their parents (Ephesians 6:2)? Is it more important for parents to instruct their children in the home (Ephesians 6:4), or for believers to instruct each other in the assembled body (Colossians 3:16)? They are all equally important and equally imperative duties. Scripture doesn't rank them.

But, someone might say, doesn't Galatians 6:10 indicate that we are to do good to all men, *especially* to those who are of the household of faith? Isn't this establishing a principle that we always meet the needs of believers before we meet the needs of unbelievers? No, it is establishing the fact that because we have a unique kind of relationship to other believers, we will be sensitive to their needs and act to meet them. It is quite possible that Paul is subtly exhorting the rigid, legalistic Galatians to do something financially for their poor brethren in Jerusalem.[1] Note well, however, that he clearly underscores the overriding responsibility of doing good to all men—believers and unbelievers. There will be times when the church will feel compelled to do good especially to those who are *not* of the household of faith but are in dire need (for example, victims of a flood, famine, or other disaster).

Second, each aspect of the church and its ministry is important. We can't say that evangelism is more important than edification, that baptism is more important than communion, that unity is more important than purity, that clergy are more important than laity. We can't say it, because the Bible doesn't say it. It says that each of these areas is significant in the life of the church. They may not all be important to you right now. They may not all be pertinent to your church at this time. But in the ongoing life of a church, all of them will have significance.

Third, the items listed in the church segment are not complete. We could add other elements such as growth, false teaching, missions, excommunication, hospitality, constitutions, liturgy, polity, ordination, children, disciplining, deaconnesses, buildings, and a host of other topics. Any one of them could then be expanded and explored. Elders, for example: their qualifications, duties, number, length of service, payment, method of selection, and discipline. The church is a complex organization and organism.

Fourth, the New Testament is replete with church truth. Hundreds of verses in the Gospels, Acts, the Epistles, and Revelation tell us what ought to be happening in and through the local church. I am grateful to God that He has seen fit to give us such a wealth of explicit information about how the body is to operate. But I am also conscious of the fact that there are problems inherent in possessing an abundance of good data. It's like having a large body of clear, deep water. It's a great place to swim. It's also easy to drown. Let me show you what I mean.

Promoting a Priority Structure

Take a lot of interesting, informative truth. Mix in a group of highly motivated people. You know what you have? A church! You know what else you have? The potential for a priority structure. Because in order to mix truth and people together effectively you must have plenty of meetings, studying, praying, planning, giving, and working. This takes time. Blend in large quantities of time with your meaningful truth and excited people and you have the makings of a high priority situation. Label all of this "commitment to God" and you have the church firmly settled in first place—top priority. Function in this mode for a few months and guess what happens? That's right, you start neglecting other responsibilities, and slowly but surely your life gets out of biblical balance. Too much of a good thing can be bad. You can drown in clear, clean, pure water.

The solution? Set up rigid policies that prohibit anyone in the body from being over-involved in the church. Enforce these policies. Make no exceptions. Instead of violating the policy, postpone or terminate the program. A balanced life is more important than a busy church. This is not to say that you should institute a "one job per person" policy. Some people have more time to invest in the church. Singles, for example, or those who are widowed, retired, or disabled. Nor am I advocating just one meeting per week. This is simply a pointed reminder that there are other things in the Christian life besides church.

Cutting down on involvement is one part of the solution, but that won't guarantee that people will either stop neglecting other biblical responsibilities or start fulfilling them. What will? A church that is thoroughly committed to preparing its people to live biblically in all of the other top priority areas. Let's examine this in greater detail.

Preparing People for Life

The church has a double focus. One is *internal*, to prepare its people for service in the body. There is, therefore, a need for training leaders, teachers, committee chairmen, committee members, ushers, musicians, sponsors, officers, group leaders, and other church workers. There is also a need for insight on Bible study, doctrine, fellowship, worship, baptism, communion, gifts, and other components of the church.

The other focus is *external*, preparing the people for life outside the church, providing wisdom and motivation for each person in relation to himself, God, family, job, government, and the world system. We can get so caught up with our internal focus, so intent on producing first class choir members, dependable ushers, cheerful givers, and ardent worshipers that we may end up giving only slight attention to our equally important external responsibilities. The church is not an end in itself. Nothing is an end in itself, except the glory of God. The church should play a strategic role in equipping us to reach that goal in every area of our lives.

This means that much of what goes on in the internal program of the church is to be directly related to the external life of its people. We teach young people about dating and mate selection and sex. We prepare them for the temptations they will inevitably face. We preach about marriage and family living and in-laws and budgets and aging parents. We discuss singleness, divorce, and remarriage. The church equips its people to function biblically in the family.

We inculcate in young people the capacity to handle homework, peer pressure, grades, cheating, popularity, athletics, school rules, and all the other things that go with their education. Administrators, teachers, and coaches may be in our congregation. They need biblical insight too. We are sensitive to the vocational calling and needs of each of our members. We are careful to avoid the "insidious double standard which speaks of clergy having a call to the ministry and other people getting a job."[2] We deal with what kinds of profits are legitimate, career mobility, ambition, risk taking, and issues pertinent to those employed in multinational companies, to those in labor unions, law enforcement, and military service. The church prepares its people to do what is right in school and on the job.

We help people struggle with whether one can be a faithful Christian and a successful politician. We help voters think through issues biblically. We help civil servants grapple with the pressure to compromise. When we pray in the Sunday morning worship service for "those in authority over us" we take a moment before to intelligently comment on who they are and what they need. The church alerts its members to their civic responsibilities.

Our church members are in the world—every week. They need to be equipped to handle temptation, television, gambling, advertising, pornography, news, materialism, recreation, entertainment, humanism, immorality, hedonism, sales, movies, secularism, and all the other things that Satan uses to confuse and corrupt us. They also need to know when and how to penetrate that world with the gospel and when to withdraw from that world to avoid contamination. The church equips its people to know how to handle their world—when to flee, when to fight.

Think About It

How can the church prepare its people to live competently and consistently in these significant areas? We can start by *thinking*. We haven't been, says Harry Blamires, and as a result "no vital Christian mind plays fruitfully, as a coherent and recognizable influence, upon our social, political, or cultural life."[3] We have "succumbed to the secular drift with a degree of weakness and nervelessness unmatched in Christian history."[4] The church has suffered what Blamires calls "a complete loss of intellectual morale."[5]

Why? Two reasons. First, we withdraw from these other areas of life, and the more we isolate from them, the less we think about them. Second, we devote much of our critical thinking to developing and maintaining the church's internal program. This is all well and good, but we need to think beyond the church's internal program. We need to get clergy and laity together on a consistent basis in "think tanks"—to probe and articulate how the Word of God relates to the issues of family, school, work, politics, government, and the world system. This can be done at pastor's conferences, at lay retreats, in men's groups, in women's groups, in the church staff, in the church boards, in family units, or singles groups. We could form an "Outward Bound" committee which would devote itself exclusively to hammering out guidelines for believers in one or more of these areas of life. Members could read and discuss significant books. Or they could call in competent resource individuals from the congregation and the community to stimulate thinking.

You know what you will find? That a few people are already doing a lot of thinking in one or more of these areas. They are hammering out a biblical philosophy of work. Or of citizenship. Encourage them! Use them! You will also find that some have almost totally succumbed to secular, humanistic thinking. Rescue and redirect them. Then you will find some who don't like to think deeply about their marriage, their work, their government, their world. They gently but firmly need to be led to do this. Not because it is fashionable, but because it is biblical.

Talk About It

Now, what do we do with all of this good thinking? We *communicate* it. We run a series of elective classes on Christian citizenship or on discovering our God-given talents. We preach a series of sermons on the Christian's attitude toward the natural environment or what it means for believers to reprove the unfruitful works of darkness in River City. We provide qualified counseling in the realm of vocational guidance and financial planning and sexual obsessions. We have sections in the church library that feature books on the world, government, family, work, church, and self. We require the reading of them. (Well, maybe we've gone too far!)

We let the seasoned older members teach the younger ones (Titus 2:1-8). We gather data on new members that includes not only what they can do in the church but what they do outside the church. In the pastoral prayer we pray not only for the sick and the foreign missionaries, but also for the assembly line workers who struggle with the boredom that tedious, repetitive work brings. And for the business executive who will be making crucial decisions this coming week. We gather a group of lay people around the pastor and let them help him prepare his sermon. He is a specialist in the truth. They specialize in different facets of life.

We set our sights to relate biblical truth to every person, every profession, every age, every socio-economic level, both sexes. Gibbs comments on the fact that "so much of our Christian adult education work is 'middle, middle, middle'— just for people who are middle-aged, middle class, and of middle ability."[6] We might add that the truth we serve them is middle-of-the-road.

To help integrate truth into life, we dip aggressively into the crucible of human experience for illustrations and applications. We illumine minds, mobilize feelings, and motivate decisions by linking the Word of God to the classroom, the playing field, the laboratory, the gymnasium, the parked car. We filter these truths into the shop, the office, the store, the checkout counter, the delivery truck, the kitchen, the bedroom, the freeway, the RV, the boat, the ski lift, and the bowling alley. We take into account we are talking with people who are apathetic, frustrated, worried, challenged, excited, happy, preoccupied, wealthy, poor, addicted, or hostile. We listen to them and find out where they're at, and then we show them where they can and ought to be.

We use creative methods that will insert the truth into life. We dramatize the discussion two students have with each other about the grades they got on the tests that were just returned. We vocalize the internal dialogue a woman has with herself as she decides whether she will return the extra five dollar bill the clerk inadvertently gave her. We role-play the heated argument a teenager has with her parents about how late she can stay out. We set up a case study that allows salesmen to interact with the temptation of padding their expense accounts, or whether they should tell the boss about another salesman who is. We let people solve the problem of whether they will park in the space designated for the handicapped (even though they are not), since they are in a hurry, and it's close to the entrance, and all they need is a loaf of bread. We'll develop a slide presentation of a day in the life of Henrietta Housewife or Sally Secretary or Collegiate Carl or Businessman Bryce or Retired Ralph. We'll have a narrator comment on the pressures associated with each scene, and we'll have the audience determine what a biblical response would be.

J. B. Phillips said it: "If words are to enter men's hearts and bear fruit, they must be the right words shaped cunningly to pass men's defences and explode silently and effectually within their minds." Use methods that will light fuses.

Do It!

We think about it. We talk about it. We do it. The truth that transforms is to be transmitted. We ask probing questions in class. We are willing to state our Christian position on an issue. We don't play dirty, even when our opponent does. We quit at 5:00 P.M. and go home, even though we haven't done everything that needs to be done. We empty the wastebaskets and vacuum the rug—spontaneously. We raise our standard of giving, rather than our standard of living. We read something besides the comics; for example, the editorial page. We run for the school board, because we realize it is just as important as serving on the church board. We campaign for a candidate we believe in. We write letters to legislators. And television advertisers. We learn to appreciate good music, beautiful art, and the natural world around us. And, along with all of these . . . we go to church.

We'll build in some accountability. Bill will report back to Tom how he handled the tensions between himself and his boss last week. Fran will give Martha a call to tell her how she is coping with her stubborn five year old. Fred and Molly will share with their growth group how they are doing in their commitment to communicate better with each other. Herb will feel free to corner Tony now and then and ask him how he is handling the desire to read pornographic material and sneak into an adult movie. Christianity is not a do-it-by-yourself religion.

By the Way . . .

All of the preceding thoughts are firmly rooted in Scripture. Look at Paul's words in Titus 2:11-12:

> For the grace of God has appeared, bringing
> salvation to all men, instructing us to deny
> ungodliness and worldly desires and to live

> sensibly, righteously and godly in the present
> age. . . .

Notice what grace does. It saves and instructs. It redeems lives and it renews minds. It puts you on the team and teaches you how to play the game.

The church is one primary place where this instruction takes place. The training program has a double thrust. First, we learn to deny ungodliness and worldly lusts. *Deny* means to reject or repudiate. It is translated *disown* in Acts 3:13 (NASB). It is in the aorist tense, showing the necessity of a deliberate, decisive act. The church must teach its people what constitutes ungodliness and worldly lusts and it must teach them how to boldly and effectively reject these things. Denying involves both pointing out sin and giving up sin. There is (we hope) not a lot of ungodliness and worldly lust in the church, so the responsibility to deny sin is carried out within our own lives and in relationships with others. We are to be actively against sin. We cannot accomplish this just sitting in church.

There is a positive thrust, too. We are to be trained to live sensibly, righteously, and godly in the present age. "Age" refers to a period of time. It can mean eternity, it can mean the past, it can mean the future, but here it is qualified to mean the present—*right now.* Right now! In your present home situation. In your junior year at school. In your current job. With the Republicans in office. With the "no right turn on red" sign at that often deserted intersection. With inflation and taxes going up. With surgery coming next week. With nuclear weapons a major issue. With a leak in the roof. God wants Christians who will contextualize their faith. The church ought to be training Christians to do this sensibly, righteously, and godly. While we are looking for the second coming of Christ (Titus 2:13), we are to be training and living, practicing and playing, in the class and in the lab, huddling and running the plays—denouncing what is wrong, doing what is right.

Chapter Twelve, Notes

[1]Alan Cole, *The Epistle of Paul to the Galatians, The Tyndale New Testament Commentaries* (Grand Rapids: Wm. B. Eerdmans Publishing Company, 1965), pp. 177-179. Cole argues convincingly for this, calling attention to Galatians 2:10, 6:6-9, Romans 15:27, and 2 Corinthians 9:6 as supporting evidence.

[2]Mark Gibbs, *Christians With Secular Power* (Philadelphia: Fortress Press, 1981), p. 8. By "secular power" Gibbs refers to those who hold significant decision-making positions in the secular world. He provides insight on how the church can equip its members who are in politics, business and industry, labor unions, police and military, and the media.

[3]Harry Blamires, *The Christian Mind* (Ann Arbor, Mich.: Servant Books, 1963), p. vii.

[4]Ibid. p. 3.

[5]Ibid.

[6]Gibbs, *Christians With Secular Power*, p. 54.

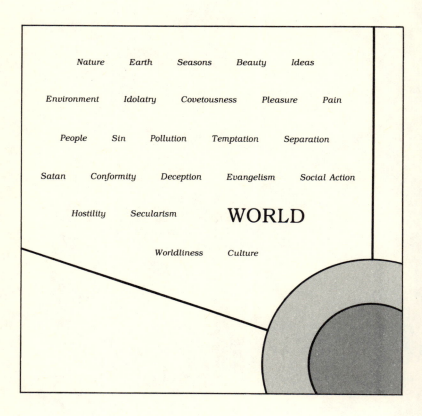

Nature   Earth   Seasons   Beauty   Ideas

Environment   Idolatry   Covetousness   Pleasure   Pain

People   Sin   Pollution   Temptation   Separation

Satan   Conformity   Deception   Evangelism   Social Action

Hostility   Secularism   WORLD

Worldliness   Culture

CHAPTER THIRTEEN

You and the World

Expanding Awareness

Last but not least on our list is the world. It's a small word but a large subject. What we intend to do is create a bigger and better perspective of the biblical concept of the world. We've begun at the left by identifying some of the many factors in it.

Perspective

As developed in Scripture, *world* has a variety of meanings. It refers to the created world of nature, to the developed world of things, to the arena of satanic control, and to the human beings who live here. The world is complex. This is the first element of perspective we need.

Second, the world is important. It is just as important as the church or the family. For example, the exhortation to "stand firm against the schemes of the devil" (Ephesians 6:11) is as important as the exhortation to be "showing forbearance to one another in love" (Ephesians 4:2). In his first letter, Peter discusses Christian responsibilities in government, work, and family and then moves on into the world. He tells Christians that they are in a hostile world, and they can expect to be intimidated, slandered, reviled, and interrogated. They should not only be able to explain what they believe but they also should be prepared to suffer for their stand (1 Peter 2-4). These "world" truths are no less significant than the government, work, and family truths.

Notice how Peter puts church, self, and world together in chapter 5. Verses 1 through 5 instruct church leaders and those who follow them. Verses 6 and 7 talk to individual believers about their humility, exaltation, and anxiety. Verses 8 and 9 comment on how to handle the devil. There is no priority sequence here; it is all equally applicable truth. Note further how all of these truths are linked to God.

Third, each item in the world segment is important. As you browse through the list, I'm sure you identify more strongly with certain ones at this time in your life. You might be a college student and say that temptation is "where it's at for me." You may be involved in an urban ministry and be keyed in on social action. You might be one who is taking a strong stand for your faith at the office and encountering a lot of hostility.

That doesn't mean that temptation, social action, and hostility are essentially more important items; it does mean that they are more germane to one person's life right now. That's the way life is: certain things are always on the front burner, but life is a big stove, with lots of things cooking! To use another analogy, life is like a golf bag full of clubs. Which club is most important? It depends on where you are. If you're teeing off on a long hole, the driver is most important. If you're on the green, the putter is most important. If you're in the lake . . . well, the ability to recover (your ball or your composure) is most important. All the clubs in the bag are important, but they are not all pertinent to every situation. All the biblical truths concerning the world are significant. We must know them so that we can use them when we need them.

Fourth, the world is like the air we breathe—it is everywhere. It touches our personal lives, our homes, our work, our government, even our churches. When you go home you don't shut out the world. When you go to church you don't leave the world. Our responsibility is to know how to live in the world without being a part of it (John 17:14-19).

What Is the World?

As shown in the circle below, the world is nature, people, and things. By *nature* we mean all that God originally created—the heavens, the earth, darkness, light, sun, moon, stars and planets, animals, gravity, water, air, color, beauty, seasons, atoms, molecules, elements, and so on. It is the world of Genesis 1, Psalm 8, Psalm 19, Isaiah 40, and Colossians 1:16-17.

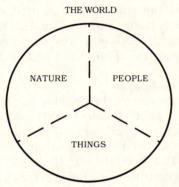

THE WORLD

NATURE   PEOPLE

THINGS

By *people* we mean human beings. This includes both sexes, all ages, every race, color, every religion, every generation. This is the world of people that God created (Genesis 1-2), the world of people that God loves (John 3:16), and the world of people for whom Christ died (1 John 2:2).

By *things* we mean that which comes into being when people interact with each other and with nature. A man and a woman interact with each other, fall in love, and bring into being a thing called marriage. A teacher and students interact with each other and bring into being a thing called learning. A group of individuals interact with each other and bring into being a thing called a team.

People not only interact with each other; they interact with nature. People interact with the color and design in nature and produce a thing called art. They use things such as wood, leather, clay, metal, and pigments to do this. Others interact with the substance and laws of nature to produce things in the realm of science. Some interact with the order and structure in nature to create a thing called mathematics, which has resulted in things called computers. People interact with distance and produce things called transportation. We interact with minerals and produce things called metal, out of which we make things called buildings, cars, boats, planes. We interact with sounds and bring into being that thing called music. As people interact with each other and nature over a period of time, they formulate a thing called culture.

Things, then, as we are using the term, refers to words, ideas, relationships, objects, attitudes, actions, organizations, institutions, and the like. But there is one thing we haven't yet mentioned—sin. The world of nature, people, and things isn't neutral. If not, then what is it?

The World, Sin, and Satan

In its original form the world of nature and people was classified as "very good" (Genesis 1:31). At that point, good people worked with a good natural world and brought into being good things. Then Satan and sin entered the picture (Genesis 3:1-6). That brought into the world of people and nature a curse and corruption (Genesis 3:7-24). Now we have sinful people interacting with each other and with a natural world that is often eccentric, at times even belligerent. The "things" we produce are not always good.

The world of nature, people, and things is now enemy-occupied territory. Satan is designated as the "god" and the "ruler" of this world (2 Corinthians 4:4, John 12:31, 16:11); consequently, the whole world lies in the power of the evil one (1 John 5:19). This means that our world is profoundly permeated by satanic influence—a defiling, deceptive scheme that is at work around us and in us; designed to convince us to conform to a mindset and a lifestyle that are essentially anti-God and pro-self.[1]

At the heart of this self-centered, satanic scheme are covetousness and idolatry. According to Scripture, they are both significant and they go together (Ephesians 5:5, Colossians 3:5, Romans 7:7-8, Exodus 20:3-6, 17). What we idolize, we covet. What we covet, we idolize.

The world inspires us to covet a "thing" called success or status. But in order to achieve it, we may have to go deeply in debt, neglect our spouse, alienate some friends, and compromise our values. That's how the satanic system gets to us. We covet new appliances, sleek automobiles, the latest fashions, a 4.0 grade point average, a trim figure. These "things" aren't inherently wrong, but when we make idols of them, we're in trouble.

We idolize new houses and tear up beautiful natural wooded areas to build them. We idolize new products and large profits, pollute the air and the water to manufacture them, and use questionable advertising techniques to manipulate the public into buying them. We idolize people and let them run (even ruin) our lives.

The naive, illiterate pagan worships a tree, a mountain, a river, a stone figure, a carved stick. The educated, sophisticated pagan worships campers, computers, coupons, cable TV, calories, and credit.

The Christian and Nature

Christians know how to relate to the world of nature. We know everything in it was created by God and that it is very good (Genesis 1:31, Acts 17:24). We know it is our responsibility to fill it, subdue it, and rule over it (Genesis 1:28). We recognize that this divinely ordained stewardship means we are to be interested in ecology, environment, field burning, strip mining, emission control, reforestation, pesticides, soil erosion, and endangered species. We are also sensitive to the aesthetic qualities of the natural world—color, size, shape, proportion, design, harmony, variety, creativity, symmetry, balance, majesty, awesomeness. If anyone ought to appreciate beauty, certainly it should be the Christian. We do these things not to idolize the creation but to worship the Creator.

Furthermore, the Christian should be aware that nature is both consistent and erratic, erratic because of the effects of the curse. We know that there will be earthquakes, tornadoes, lightning, floods, drought, ice storms, and heat waves. When these events occur, they bring tragedy into our world, even into our own lives. We do not respond with anger or fatalism, but with a sober reflection on the gravity of sin, the reality of judgment, and most assuredly, the fact that *nothing* shall separate us from the love of God (Romans 8:35-39).

The Christian and People

"All men will know that you are my disciples if you meet on Sundays at 11:00 A.M. and 6:00 P.M."[2] We often act as though that is what Christ said. But it isn't. He said that the world would get the message if Christians love each other (John 13:35).

Lost people need to see God's goodness in action. Christians are to act to meet that need (Matthew 5:16, Philippians 2:15, 1 Peter 2:12). A holy lifestyle will facilitate the convicting work of the Spirit as He makes the unbeliever aware of sin, righteousness, and judgment (John 16:8-11). People need to see and hear goodness. Regardless of their attitude and response, we are to be "zealous for what is good" (1 Peter 3:13). We cannot adequately accomplish this at a distance. We are to be "above reproach *in the midst* of a crooked and perverse generation" (Philippians 2:15).

Lost people need to find Christ. We are God's ambassadors, communicating the word of reconciliation (2 Corinthians 5:18-21). To do this, we must be willing to get close to people, so close and so attractive that they ask us questions: questions we are ready to answer (Colossians 4:5-6, 1 Peter 3:15). God loves the world of people and so must we (John 3:16).

Yet we walk an interpersonal tightrope when it comes to our relationships with unbelievers. While witnessing to them, we are to steer clear of entangling alliances with them. We are not to be "unequally yoked" with unbelievers, nor are we to "participate" in their "unfruitful deeds of darkness" (2 Corinthians 6:16-18, Ephesians 5:7-11). A "yoke" is present where there is an equal, binding relationship such as marriage or a business partnership. When a believer is yoked to an unbeliever, their differing values and goals will create conflicts and compromise. God's counsel is: Don't do it! What we aim for is communication without compromise, separation without isolation.

The Christian and Things

Remember now, "things" means more than the stuff you have in your junk drawer. This term refers to all that comes into being when people interact with each other and with the natural world. Relationships, products, organizations, ideas, for example. What is to be the Christian's attitude toward these *things*? A quick reply could well be that we are not to love the world, nor the *things* that are in the world (1 John

2:15). That seems to sum it up. Or does it? Let's take a moment to look at the biblical doctrine of *things.*

"*Everything* created by God is *good.*" That's what Paul told Timothy, and he illustrated his point by referring to marriage and food, two things that come into being as people relate to each other and nature (1 Timothy 4:1-5). Later, he reminded Timothy that this same God "richly supplies us with *all things to enjoy*" (1 Timothy 6:17). There he was talking about money. Money, marriage, and food are good things to be enjoyed. As we explore the biblical doctrine of things we find that all things are pure, all things are clean, all things are lawful, all things are from God. Nothing is unclean of itself; there is no such thing as an idol.[3]

To see "things" in this light requires a mind renewed by the Holy Spirit and the Word of God. Christians can develop this kind of mindset (Romans 12:2; 8:5-6). We can filter out and strip away sinful attitudes and actions with regard to "things." In their refined, revised state we can see them as good and enjoy them and use them for the glory of God. We can appreciate good music, we can enjoy comfortable furniture, we can employ the latest technology, we can avidly pursue a hobby, we can get an education, we can hike and hunt and fish and invest and talk and travel and study and give and plan and . . . As long as they are within the will of God, we can do and enjoy many, many things. That's because, as Solomon wisely said, they are all ultimately a gift from the hand of God (Ecclesiastes 2:24-25, 5:18-20). A God who says, "Whether you eat or drink or whatever you do, do all to the glory of God" (1 Corinthians 10:31). That little word "all" not only *cautions* us to do what is right, but *challenges* us to discover new "things" that will glorify God.

But the Christian has to be very careful, because as Robert Frost wrote, "things are in the saddle and ride mankind." Satan is seeking to cinch that saddle up as tight as he can. We are enticed to worship the creature rather than the Creator (Romans 1:25), to lust after the things of the world rather than love the Father (1 John 2:15-17), to love money so much that when we get some it inflates our ego and becomes our primary source of security (1 Timothy 6:10, 17). We have to guard against being so friendly with the world that our relationship has to be classified as adultery and our attitude toward God as one of hostility (James 4:4). We have to watch out for this thing called anger, for when we let it smolder, we're letting the devil get his foot in the door (Ephesians 4:26-27).

The world is a treadmill, and we are on it, being swept backward if we aren't consciously walking forward. Satan loves to raise the treadmill up so that it becomes harder and harder for us to walk in the Spirit, easier and easier to slip back into the flesh. At times we wish we could get off the treadmill and hibernate, but that's not an option. We're here to stay. Resident aliens—that's what we are. But we have more than adequate resources. God provides us with the offensive and defensive weapons we need to stand firm and resist the schemes of the devil (Ephesians 6:10-20). With His wisdom and power we can handle "things" properly. We can explore the potential of the world of things: discover them, use them, and enjoy them without being entrapped by them. At the same time we can resist the pressure to conform to this world and expose the sin that is in the world, for "greater is He who is in you than he who is in the world" (1 John 4:4).

By the Way . . .

Why don't priority lists mention the world or Satan? Because priority lists accentuate the positive. If they were more complete they would also list the relationships we are to avoid and the things we are not to do. And what would be at the top of the list? Would it be the flesh? The world? Satan? Murder? Idolatry?

I won't belabor the point. You get the picture. A sequential listing of negative priorities would be just as absurd as the positive lists we dealt with earlier in the book.

Chapter Thirteen, Notes

[1]Defiling—2 Peter 1:4, 2:20; James 1:27; deceptive—2 Corinthians 11:14-15; Revelation 12:9; scheme—Ephesians 6:11; conform—Romans 12:2. Other verses which are pertinent are 1 Peter 5:8, Ephesians 1:1-3, 6:12, 16, Isaiah 14:12-14.

[2]Joseph C. Aldrich, *Life-Style Evangelism* (Portland, Ore.: Multnomah Press, 1981), p. 36.

[3]This enlightened perspective on "things" is presented in Titus 1:15, Romans 14:14, 20, 1 Corinthians 6:12, 8:4, 6.

CHAPTER FOURTEEN

A Parcel of Problems

That's the way it is—a plurality of priorities. A multitude of equally significant biblical responsibilities. A lot of number one commitments. And—a whole parcel of problems. Let's briefly highlight some of them.

Time

We round off our diagram with a time line. The outer circle represents the time we have to discharge our biblical responsibilities. That circle is the same size for all of us. We each have twenty-four hours a day, seven days a week, fifty-two weeks per year. Time is not elastic; that is, we can't stretch a day into something longer than twenty-four hours.

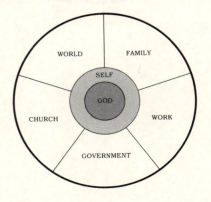

Yet, in a way, time is elastic. Look what happens to the person who devotes large amounts of time to his work and small amounts of time to his family.

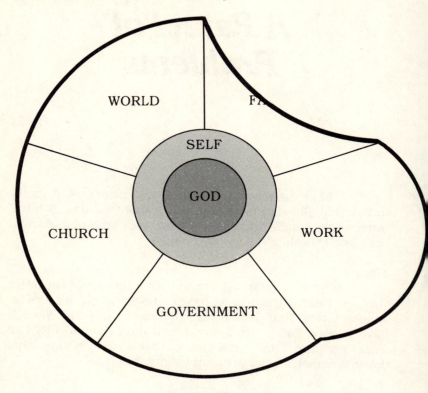

Or how about the individual who overindulges in church activities and spends little or no time with unbelievers?

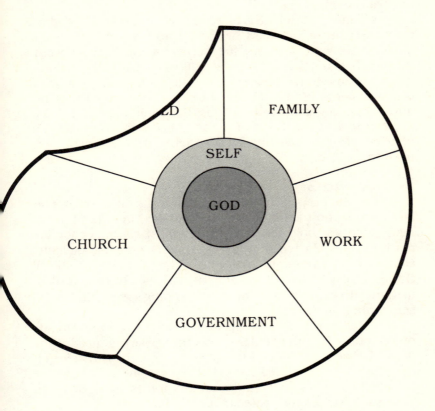

We may get so fixed on one area that we neglect everything else. Life becomes like a tire with a bald spot that is ballooning and ready to blow out. That makes the going rough. For everybody. Long before the blowout.

The point is obvious. When you invest a lot of extra time in one area of life, you have to withdraw an equal amount of time from other areas. When you do that, you can get out of balance because it takes time to discharge biblical responsibilities. If you don't spend time with unbelievers, you can't witness to them and you won't win them. If you don't spend time with your kids, you will neglect your responsibility to nurture and train them.

Time in Scripture is more than chronology. It is opportunity. Scripture counsels Christian to walk wisely, and we are told that the way to do this is to redeem or make the most of our time (Ephesians 5:15-17). Time is like ripe fruit. If you don't use it, you lose it. Remember, our basic diagram is not a set of time segments. Some relationships and responsibilities require large, regular blocks of time. Schedule yourself to take the time to do those things. You can't master the clock. It ticks on relentlessly. You can master your schedule. It does what you tell it to do.

Overcommitment

Some people can't say no. They take on too many relationships and too many responsibilities. They enroll in too many courses, hold down too many jobs, volunteer for too many tasks, make too many appointments, serve on too many committees, have too many friends. They are trying to be all things to all men all at once all by themselves. They equate dedication with exhaustion. They end up doing some things well, some things poorly.

Bombarded with requests? Learn to say no! Already overcommitted? Cut back! See something else that needs to be done? Delegate it! That's what the leaders of the early church did. The widows needed food. The congregation needed the Word. The leaders resisted the temptation to try to do both. They said "No" and delegated (Acts 6:1-6).

> Yes, yes, yes we say,
>   without a thought for the day.
> Running and fretting to make ends meet,
>   rushing from Suzie to Joe and to Pete.
> Our lives, in upheaval, have turned to a tizzy,
>   never completing, because we're too busy.
> All we must do for a tranquil soul,
>   is employ a word, just one, called *NO*.
>   (Author unknown)

Involved in too many good things? You are either trying to please men or trying to play God, or both.

Inefficiency

The problem is not always overcommitment. Often it is underefficiency and lack of discipline. To use time wisely connotes efficiency. But we are often satisfied with mediocrity. We are easily distracted; we complicate the simple; our efforts are often haphazard and random. We ramble through our days allowing ourselves to be dominated by incidentals and infatuated with trivialities. Our estimations are off the mark. ("Sure, I can do this in an hour.") Our trips aren't always well-planned. ("Oh, my, I've got to go back home and get the empty milk bottles.") At best we are erratic. At worst we are inefficient.

We need to get serious and practical about redeeming the time. Learn to type. Take speed reading. Get a pocket calculator. Invest in a word processor or even a computer. Hire an expert rather than muddle through for hours or days. Plan your trips to the shopping center. Map out what you are going to say before you dial the number. Do more planning and then discipline yourself to live according to the plan. Otherwise, you'll be another hapless victim of Parkinson's law: Work expands to fill all the available time you have to do it. It will, but you can bend that trend with more careful attention to time, motion, speed, duplication, combination, and a host of other things pertinent to efficiency.

Even in his day the apostle Paul was interested in an efficient lifestyle. He lived like a man running a race—aiming at a specific goal; or like a man engaged in a fight—refusing to swing wildly, not wanting to waste a single punch (1 Corinthians 9:24-27). The Bible condemns the laziness of the sluggard, commends order and structure, and encourages a sensible, disciplined approach to life.[1] Each one of us has a multitude of biblical responsibilities. When they aren't being done well, or on time, or are left undone, there's often one basic reason—sloppiness.

Interruptions

A student sticks his head in at my door and says, "Hey prof, have you got a minute?" Actually I don't. I'm preparing materials for a class that meets in thirty minutes. But he looks worried. Which is more important, one worried student seeking counsel right now, or twenty-five students expecting quality instruction thirty minutes from now? That's the way life is. Every day unexpected, unplanned intrusions interrupt my schedules. It may be sickness, an accident, surprise visitors, a phone call, a letter. Does faithfulness mean that I stick unswervingly to my plans? Or does it mean that I seek to respond immediately to every opportunity that crosses my path?

Romans 8:28 speaks to this issue. It says that God causes all things to work together for a good purpose. Emergencies and interruptions fit into "all things." What good purpose could God have for letting us experience these intrusions? At least two. First, God may be at work to test our commitment to our already established schedules. The Word of God tells us to be "steadfast." The God of the Word may allow intrusions to come our way to test and develop our steadfastness. He wants us to learn to "stick with the plan" and not let a cacophonous medley of circumstances run our lives.

Second, God may be at work testing our ability to flex to meet needs. Burden bearing is in every Christian's job description. Sometimes we see these opportunities coming; sometimes they blind-side us. It is at the point of encounter that we have to discern whether our schedule or their need is more important. I must quickly determine if the worried student needs immediate attention or if he can come back later while I go ahead with my plan to prepare for class. We must develop a rigid flexibility!

Private vs. Public

We tend to work on the public areas and let the private areas slide. We must mask negative attitudes with positive actions.

Bill and Bonnie and the children arrive at the church on Sunday morning. They park and walk hand in hand toward the educational building, smiling and greeting their many friends. They carry their Bibles. They appear happy, peaceful, and friendly. They contribute to the discussion in Sunday school class. Bonnie shares a prayer request. Bill gives a word of personal testimony. The family sits together in church, giving rapt attention to all that takes place. In the narthex, they greet visitors, inquire about Tom's health, encourage the pastor, and promise to pray for Mrs. Johnson's surgery on Wednesday. Their public image is impeccable.

But what happens in the car on the way home when Susie starts whining, and her brother Todd kicks her, and another motorist on the freeway cuts in front of Bill, and Bonnie "evaluates" the soloist in the morning service? And what happens inside their home? What are they watching on TV? What magazines are they reading? Do they ever read or study the Bibles they carry on Sunday? Is Bill's reputation at the office in harmony with his reputation in his Sunday school class?

Man looks on the outward appearance (1 Samuel 16:7). We know this and tend to cater to it. God looks at both. The words of our mouth (public) and the meditations of our heart (private) are both to be acceptable in His sight (Psalm 19:14). Both our public and private lives need to be in harmony with the Word of God.

Material Possessions

How do cars, boats, houses, bikes, skis, and stereos fit into the diagram we have been using? Well, we could put them in the center, in place of God. But obviously that's not right. We could create another outer segment and label it "material possessions", but we know that our responsibility is to love people, not inanimate objects. And our responsibility is to seek first the kingdom of God and His righteousness, rather than focus our attention on food, clothing, and shelter (Matthew 6:25-34).[2]

It is best for us to regard material possessions as *means* to accomplish the task of loving God, self, and others. A house provides protection and comfort for the family. It also gives us a place to fellowship with members of the body and to cultivate relationships with unsaved friends and relatives. We can use a boat to meet our need for recreation, relaxation, and meditation. We must be careful, however. Means easily become ends, and when that happens we go beyond using things and start worshiping them. When we want bigger and better and more things we are tipping toward idolatry.

Individual Differences

Ever since you brought me home from the bookstore, I've been watching you closely. You're different. Not different/ weird, but different/unique. For example, you always put me back on the shelf in the same place. You're well organized. Then there's the way you pause and reread certain sentences, and then underline them. You're a probing, analytic thinker. Then there was the day I watched you through the open doorway, fixing the kitchen plumbing. Or should I say, trying to fix the plumbing? I agree, that's not your area of strength. I've been observing your wife, too. In many areas you two are different from each other. She's artistic and very practical. You're athletic and a bit theoretical. She loves a crowd. You love a book.

You're different. We all are. We are each "one of a kind". Now get this: *This means that each of us will live the Christian life differently.* Each of us will work out our salvation according to our divinely designed personal distinctives.

Because of personality, education, experience, spiritual gifts, and natural talents, each one of us will tend to gravitate toward certain areas and away from others. We are more comfortable in certain relationships; more capable in certain responsibilities. You may be very creative, and channel these skills into your local church. Your spouse may be an adept problem solver, and employ these skills in the home. A friend may be singularly equipped with an analytic mind and the ability to persuade. He may use these proficiencies in politics or in a teaching profession.

Each of us is unique. None of us are totally competent. All of us have strengths and limitations. Therefore we will be more interested and more proficient in some things, and less concerned and less capable in others. But this doesn't give us the right to be unconcerned or incompetent in any area of biblical responsibility. We need to develop biblical competency in all areas, realizing that we will go on to excel in some things and not in others.

Intimacy

Don't equate intimacy with importance. That's one of the reasons we continue to have lists of priorities: we think that the more intimate the relationship, the more important it is. So we put God first on the list because of the intimate nature of our relationship with Him, and family second because of the strong, intimate bonds present there. We put unbelievers down near the bottom because we know we must be careful about getting too close to them. When it comes to *self* we're stumped. We aren't sure whether to put us up near the top of the list and really get next to ourselves, or assign us a berth at the bottom and steer clear of ourselves. We face this dilemma because we tend to equate intimacy with importance. We shouldn't.

Let me illustrate. It is important that I be honest with my wife when she asks what I think about our relationship. It is also important that I be honest with the Internal Revenue agent when he asks about business expenses claimed on my tax return. Do I have a more intimate relationship with my wife than with the IRS agent? You'd better believe it! Does my less intimate relationship with the IRS agent mean that I have less responsibility to be honest with him? It certainly does not. If God tells me to be honest, I am to be honest. Regardless of the level of intimacy.

Intimacy itself is necessary and significant, and is to be developed appropriately in all our relationships. But intimacy is a cunning concept. Where we don't need it, it often comes easily, such as our relationship with the world system, false teachers, and the opposite sex outside of marriage. Where it is imperative, for example, in the home and the church, it is often more difficult to develop and maintain.[3] Paul told the Corinthians not to be intimate ("bound together") with unbelievers (2 Corinthians 6:14), and in the next paragraph exhorted them to develop a deeper intimacy with him. He asked them to "make room for us in your hearts. . . . for . . . you are in our hearts to die together and to live together" (2 Corinthians 7:2-3). Satan is sly. He will promote intimacy where God prohibits it and he will thwart it where God desires it. Christians are to be close, but they are also to be careful.

Special Emphasis

At times we have to emphasize certain relationships and certain responsibilities. Why? Often because of *present needs*. Starting a new business? You may have to devote extra time to it, because it needs a higher degree of effort in the start-up phase. Recently married? Your relationship needs a lot of attention. New baby in the house? It needs a lot of care; around the clock. In a new job? You may need to bring home that brief-case for awhile. Don't have any non-Christian friends? You'll need to start inviting people over. New in the community? You'll need to spend some extra time getting acquainted. Learned a new truth? Now you need to work on applying it.

Another reason for special emphasis is *previous neglect*. Been away on a business trip? Like it or not, you've been neglecting your wife and kids. Now you need to bring things back into balance by being totally available to them for a few evenings, or maybe all weekend. Have you been neglecting regular time in the Word and prayer? Reset the alarm clock and rise to the challenge! Under conviction about some personal problems you have neglected to deal with? Take time to work on them.

But we have to be careful about all of this. Special emphasis is designed to bring us back into a biblical balance, not to unbalance us in a different direction.

This is where a "things to do" list comes in handy. We put certain things on that list because we have been neglecting to do them, or because we are now in a situation where they need to be done right away. We could call this a "priority list." But I prefer to call it a "responsibility list", signifying that everything on it needs to be done. The term *priority list* often connotes that the items near the top are important while those down the line . . . well, we'll get to them. If we can. This approach causes us to carry around a lot of unfinished lists.

Hard Choices

"Shall I go to church this evening or do my homework?" "Should I work late or go home for supper with the wife and kids?" "Should I look for a second job, or should we move to a cheaper apartment?" "Shall I go to bed early and get a good night's rest, or call Charlie and spend an hour on the phone listening to his problems?" "Should I serve as an usher at the church or serve as precinct committee person for my political party?" "Is it better to coach Little League or teach Sunday school?" "Should I volunteer for a PTA office or work on the missions committee?" "Do I go to my child's soccer game, or call on one more customer?"

If you have a neat list of sequential priorities, the decisions are not too difficult. Just check to see which option is higher on the list and go for it. But if you see your priorities encircling you—each one a God-given responsibility—then you'll have to work your way through the data very carefully, seeking to understand the will of the Lord in each decision (Ephesians 5:17).

How do you determine which one is right? You often make the choice on the basis of present need or previous neglect. Have you seldom been involved in PTA? Got a couple of kids in school now? Then do it. What about the Missions Committee? It will have to do without you while you do missions work in the PTA! Have you been promising your child that you'll come to a game sometime soon? Will he or she be glancing expectantly toward the stands hoping you'll show up? Then go. What about the sale you'll miss? Let somebody else have it. Work on it tomorrow, or forget it. Right now that little soccer player needs something money can't replace—your presence.

Obviously if you go to soccer games all the time or invest all your efforts in the PTA, you'll probably start neglecting your business or your church. Balance is the key. It's when you make the same choice time and time again that you get out of balance. Make the choices that keep you in balance and you'll be walking wisely.[4] We tend to choose what we like, what is pleasant and fun, and what is easy and convenient. But always making those choices will produce trouble with a capital *T*, because we will inevitably get out of balance by doing too much of a good thing.

By the Way . . .

Growth ought to simplify life. Right? Wrong. The more truth I assimilate, the more I am aware of what I should be and do. You know what this produces? Tension. God-imposed tension! The growing, obedient Christian will always live with this kind of pressure. The apostle Paul did. He knew the truth about heaven and wanted to go there. He knew the truth about earthly ministry and wanted to stay here. What did all that insight do to him? It caused tension. Look what he said:

> For to me, to live is Christ, and to die is gain. But if I am to live on in the flesh, this will mean fruitful labor for me; and I do not know which to choose. But *I am hard-pressed from both directions*, having the desire to depart and be with Christ, for that is very much better; yet to remain on in the flesh is more necessary for your sake (Philippians 1:21-24, italics mine).

"Hard-pressed from both directions"—these are the words of a man coping with tension—tension generated by his awareness of truth. Paul also had a deep understanding of the lost condition of his brethren in Israel, and this created "great sorrow and unceasing grief" in his heart (Romans 9:1-5). That's tension. God-imposed, unrelieved tension.

The Christian life is not problem-free, nor is it tension-free. A sequential priorities list is a valiant attempt to relieve this tension. But we have shown that this approach is neither biblical, practical, nor trouble-free. What is the answer?

The first part of the answer is to reduce unnecessary tension. Unnecessary tension is that imposed upon us by ourselves and others. Overcommitment, inefficiency, hypocrisy, and other factors we have discussed in this chapter create this uncalled for tension. We reduce it by not trying to do too much, by being more efficient, by being genuine on and off stage, and in similar ways.

The second part of the answer is to learn to live with tension—legitimate, biblical, God-imposed tension. As long as I have something left to do to become more like Christ, I will have to live with the tension that exists between what I am and what I ought to be. Paul refers to this tension in his own life in Philippians 3:12-16. He indicates that he has reached a certain level of maturity, but not total Christlikeness, so he continues to "press on." He exhorts Timothy in the same direction.

> But flee from these things, you man of God;
> and pursue righteousness, godliness, faith,
> love, perseverance and gentleness (1 Timothy
> 6:11, cf. 2 Timothy 2:22).

Pursue and *press on* are translations of the same word in the original Greek text. The word is both a hunting and a racing term, portraying an intense desire to reach a goal. The goal is righteousness, godliness, faith, love, perseverance, and gentleness. We experience tension not only because we haven't yet reached the goal, but also because the goal is at the end of a number of different tracks (self, family, work, and our other main areas). We have to run on all of them—at the same time—and win. That creates tension!

Just as we can play beautiful music only when the strings on the violin are in proper tension, so we can grow only when we are stretched from what we are to what we can be. There is no growth without tension.

Chapter Fourteen, Notes

[1]Cf. Proverbs 6:6-11, 1 Corinthians 14:40, 2 Timothy 1:7, Titus 2:2, 5, 6, 12. Further uses of the words *sober* and *self-control* in the Bible underscore the fact that the believer's life is to be free of fuzzy thinking and fragmented living.

[2]The exhortation to "seek first His kingdom, and His righteousness" (Matthew 6:33) fits in with the concept presented in Matthew 22:34-40, which we studied in chapter 4. To seek His kingdom is to put oneself under His rule. To seek His righteousness is to live according to His regulations. The one who is doing this will be functioning biblically in all of the areas we have developed.

[3]Why intimacy is difficult and how it can be developed is the subject of another book by the author which you may wish to read and study. J. Grant Howard, *The Trauma of Transparency* (Portland, Ore.: Multnomah Press, 1979).

[4]For a comprehensive treatment of how to get and use this wisdom see Garry Friesen, *Decision Making and the Will of God* (Portland, Ore.: Multnomah Press, 1980).

CHAPTER FIFTEEN

Moving Toward Equilibrium

Who's on First?

The traditional priority list is about as confusing as the old Abbott and Costello baseball routine: Who's on first, What's on second, I Don't Know's on third. While Abbott was posing these statements of fact, Costello was answering them as questions. The results were comical and chaotic.

A sequential priority list produces similar results. No matter what order you put your list in, a priority sequence resists logical explanation, runs counter to biblical revelation, and definitely generates some amusing conclusions. Lists were developed to help Christians organize, simplify, and balance their lives. But if a person really tries to understand and adhere to an ordered list, life will be fragmented, complex, and unbalanced.

Circular Reasoning

We have presented a different approach. Using the following model, we have visualized and verbalized the relationships and responsibilities that *coexist* in the believer's life.

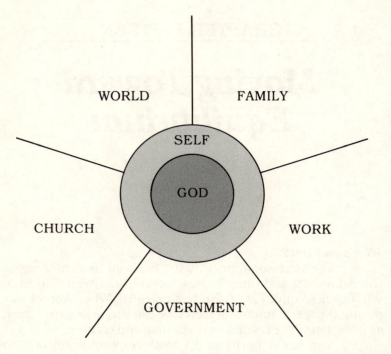

This diagram was designed to show the following:

- God wants to be central in my life. This makes knowing Him a top priority. He is important.
- God wants to be significant in my life. This makes relating His truth to every aspect of my person a top priority. I am important.
- God wants me to know and do His will in each of the relationships that surround me. This makes my responsibilities in each of these areas a top priority. They are all important.
- All of these coexist as simultaneous responsibilities rather than sequential priorities.

The preceding chapters provided biblical support for these four statements and elaborated on their practical implications.

Agree? Disagree?

Remember the agree/disagree statements in chapter 2 (p. 22)? We didn't take the time there to analyze them. But in the light of the intervening chapters I would want to rewrite each of them, because in their present form I disagree with all of them.

One way to rephrase some of them would be to say "just as important" instead of "more important." For example, Number 3 might read: "It is *just as important* for the Christian to witness as it is to eat." Or Number 4: "Family responsibilities are *just as important* as church responsibilities." What about Number 6? "Bible study and prayer are *two* of the most important responsibilities the Christian has." Number 8 is only partially true. Time alone is not enough; it is what we do with the time. We can spend the evening at home with the family, yet fail to discharge biblical responsibilities. How about Number 9? "Putting God first in my life means putting someone else last." How, I ask you, do you put someone last? It would be better to say that when God is first, others will be in their proper place, because I will know how best to relate and respond to them.

Balance

Static equilibrium. That's what we want. A state of affairs that is fixed and tranquil. Like a marble you drop into a bowl. It rolls back and forth and finally comes to rest at the bottom. That's static equilibrium. When it stops, it stays. Move it, and it quickly seeks that low point and settles down again.

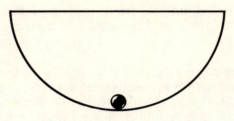

That's the kind of Christian experience we are searching for. Surely there must be some way of getting our priority into static equilibrium—settled and serene, fixed and tranquil, locked in place. But try as we may, we can't seem to find that point of restful repose. Not even a carefully devised priority list will do it. Life just isn't like a marble in a bowl.

What is it like?

Turn the bowl over. Put the marble on top at the exact point where it won't roll off in any direction. That's dynamic equilibrium. That's what life is like.

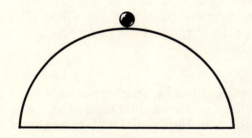

Just as gravity tugs at the marble from every side of the bowl, so a variety of biblical relationships and responsibilities tug at us from every side. If we respond properly to each one, we'll stay on top, under tension. That's why it is called *dynamic* equilibrium. If we respond improperly, or fail to respond at all, we will lose our balance and start rolling down the side. Some of us recognize that top point of balance because we go by it so often! As we mature, we will spend more time near the top of the bowl. Only Christ was in dynamic equilibrium all the time.

Guidelines

How do I stay on top? What does it take to live a balanced life? Here is what I must do.

- Acknowledge my current, biblically-significant *relationships.* Who are the important, strategic people in my life right now? It helps me to name them. God is always on the list. So am I.
- Determine my specific, biblical *responsibilities* in each of these relationships. What commandments should I be obeying now? What needs should I be meeting now? I try to single out simple, basic truths that are pertinent to current, individual needs.
- Develop a *lifestyle* within a *time schedule* that allows me to correctly and consistently discharge my biblical responsibilities in each of my current relationships. For me, lifestyle and time schedule are the two critical factors. They need each other.
- Recognize that to do all of this, I need the Spirit of God, the Word of God, and the people of God.

By the Way . . .

The main issues in the subject of priorities are first, which things in life are really important, and second, in what order should they be placed. The Scriptures make it clear that the things that are really important are God, self, and significant others (church, work, government, world, and family). Life is too complex and time is too short for us to be vague on these matters.

In what order should they be placed? Order is not a primary issue in Scripture. We are not told to do certain things in a certain order. Our responsibility is to know what God expects of us in these important areas and to arrange our lives to do His commands according to His will and thus for His glory. Don't get sidetracked. Order is not the primary issue. Obedience is.